Meditations of a Tibetan Tantric Abbot

Kensur Lekden

Translated and edited
by Jeffrey Hopkins

Associate editor:
Barbara Frye

LIBRARY OF TIBETAN WORKS & ARCHIVES

First Print 1974

Reprint 1998

ISBN: 81-85102-04-X

Published by the Library of Tibetan Works and Archives, Dharamsala-176215, India, and printed at Indraprastha Press, New Delhi-110002.

Preface

❧

Kensur Nawang Lekden (1900-71) was abbot of the Tantric College of Lower Lhasa prior to the invasion of Tibet by the Chinese Communists. At the time of the invasion, he had already been elevated to the position of "former abbot" and after fleeing to India, helped to re-establish centers of Buddhist learning and meditation in India. Events brought him to France where he tutored several monks, and in 1968 he came to the Lamaist Buddhist Monastery of America in Freewood Acres, New Jersey. In February of 1970 he was invited to teach at the Tibet House in Cambridge, Wisconsin, founded by the late Professor Richard Robinson and myself, and I served as his translator.

Kensur Rinpoche (Precious Former Abbot), an embodiment of the unified practice of sūtra and tantra and transmitter of the ancient Tibetan knowledge of meditation, taught at Tibet House for a year and a half. In a series of fifteen lectures, he set forth the paths common to sūtra and tantra, freely and intimately, as part of the transmission of Buddhism to the west. This book is comprised of those lectures. Vast from the point of view of setting forth the compassionate deeds of Bodhisattvas and profound from the point of view of presenting the empty nature of phenomena, these practices shine with the sun of Buddha's teaching reflected so brightly in snowy Tibet.

Jefrey Hopkins

Contents

❦

Contents

*Homage to Mañjuśrī and Svarasvatī.**

1
Love
❧

I want to offer good luck and happiness to you who have assembled here today.

Because all humans are doers of deeds, the Buddhist system of practice has an explanation of how to act. You do deeds by identifying that which is to be practiced or taken in hand and that which is to be forsaken or discarded. The best of what is to be adopted is making effort at the means of causing everyone to possess happiness and to be free of suffering. With respect to adopting the means of causing everyone, yourself and others, to possess happiness, there are three actions to be done: hearing, thinking and meditating.

Hearing means that you yourself hear the explanation of another or look in a book and discover what is to be done in order to obtain happiness. What will you discover with respect to possessing happiness?

First, you need to have the body of a human or a god. That body must be healthy and free of suffering. Also, you must have the resources, clothing, food, shelter and so forth of a human or a god. You must have a long life and be able to achieve what you seek.

Since we need these, what do we do in order to get them? To attain the body of a human or a god in the next birth, you must, during this lifetime, abandon the ten non-virtues and you must maintain the ten virtues. Having the body and resources of a god or a human is called high status; the low types of cyclic existence are hell beings, hungry ghosts, and animals.

The main cause of high status within cyclic existence—within the round of birth, aging, sickness and death—is good ethics, Candrakīrti says in his Supplement to (Nāgārjuna's) "Treatise on the Middle Way", "Other than ethics, there is no cause of high status." Therefore all of us living here in this world, in a former life—

* Svarasvatī is also called Sarasvatī

whenever it was—kept any of the ten virtues, and in dependence on that, we attained the present body and resources.

In determining whether our future lives will be good or not we should analyze whether our minds are presently adopting the practices which will achieve happiness. Our teacher, Śākyamuni Buddha said, "To determine what you did in the past, examine your present mind." To determine whether or not your future will be good, you should analyze the mode of behavior of your mind. The life which we have now is an effect of what we did in the past.

The cause of the arising of excellent resources—happiness and comfort—is the giving of gifts. You should not steal, you should not be miserly. Also, so that in future lives there will not be a great deal of fighting, so that you will not be punished, so that disturbances of yourself and others will not arise, you need to cultivate patience in this lifetime.

Since in the future life you need good education and knowledge of how to act, in this lifetime you must make great effort at study—at giving up what is to be abandoned and at assuming what is to be adopted. Then in order that in future lives your mind will not be distracted, in this lifetime you must cultivate meditative stabilization, samādhi, and set your mind one-pointedly.

In your next lifetime you need to be intelligent and know what is to be adopted and what is to be discarded and in order to do that, in this lifetime you need to train in the wisdom which knows what is suitable and unsuitable and in the wisdom that knows what exists. You should engage in study and training.

If the causes of happiness are achieved, the effect is happiness. Those causes of happiness are giving, ethics, patience, effort, concentration and wisdom. If in this life you are engaging in the causes of happiness—the six perfections, the ten virtues, and so forth—then in a future lifetime the effect will definitely appear, and happiness definitely will arise.

It is necessary for you to form an understanding of the practice of hearing, of what hearing is and of what is to be heard.

Then all the factors of thinking must be discovered in detail. Thinking means that you develop a conviction, that you come to the decision that for the arising of happiness, the causes of happiness and virtue must be achieved.

Because you need to obtain the happy effects and the causes which produce them, and because it is necessary for yourself and others to attain them, you must meditate. In this world there were nihilists who said that one should not meditate, doing only those activities which would bring about marvelous happiness, comfort and prosperity in this lifetime. The nihilists said that one should gather possessions and clothing, and if one's body is sick, one should take medicine, that these activities were justified, but that nothing else was needed.

Such a philosophy appeared in the world and with respect to it there is this Buddhist teaching: You need a job for your livelihood, you need to work for the sake of your country, for the sake of yourself and others, to set up factories, to plant fields; still you should act mainly for the sake of your future life, because you will not always remain in this lifetime. All persons will definitely die, and the time of death is indefinite. At the time of death nothing helps except religious practice. This is how it is. Therefore, even though you need happiness and comfort in this life and even though it is necessary to strive for the sake of food and drink now, this lifetime is short. Our longest condition of life is our countless future lives. If you consider only this which you can see now and you do not consider all the future lives which you cannot see, you will incur immeasurable fault. You will harm yourself.

What are the reasons for this? This life will definitely end. There is not even a single person in the world who will remain without dying. At the time of death not even your parents, who have been very kind to you, will go with you. You must go alone. Even if you have a family, children, brothers, sisters, friends—good friends—not even one of them can be taken along with you. It is like taking a hair out of butter; you must leave your own body as well as the place where you were lying down and go alone. Therefore you must act mainly for the welfare of future lives.

The wealth we have accumulated in this life, we cannot carry with us. The friends whom we have arranged around us, we cannot take with us. We cannot lead people with us, servants and so forth. What can be carried with us? We take with us only the predispositions of our actions; for this reason we must establish beneficial predispositions through accumulating the virtues which are the causes of happiness in the future. Therefore we must hear, think, and meditate in this lifetime for the sake of future lifetimes.

If you do not accomplish the causes of happiness in this lifetime you will not have anything at all to carry with you at the time of death.

If you have accumulated non-virtues, predispositions will have been established in your mind for the arising of suffering. If you have accumulated virtues, you will have the predispositions in your mind which give rise to happiness. It is like the body and its odor. Wherever the body goes, the odor goes with it. Just so, wherever the person goes, these causes which are the accumulations of virtue and non-virtue go with him. Therefore in this lifetime hearing must be done, and if through thinking understanding develops, meditation which achieves happiness and the causes of happiness must be performed.

You should cultivate this thought in meditation, "May happiness and the causes of happiness come to be possessed." Such meditation is of two types: meditation for your own welfare and meditation for others' welfare. If you cultivate in meditation the thought, "May I possess happiness and the causes of happiness in the next and all succeeding lifetimes," there is only a little benefit. How do you meditate so that there is great benefit? You meditate taking cognizance of the welfare of all sentient beings, thinking, "May all sentient beings throughout all of space, illustrated by my kind parents of this lifetime, possess happiness and the causes of happiness." If this meditation is done, the benefit is limitless, equal to space itself.

What example is there for the benefit? In the word of Buddha it says that if a sesame seed is squeezed, only a little bit of oil comes out, but if many are squeezed, a huge barrel can be filled with the oil. Even if you meditate only once for only five minutes taking cognizance of all sentient beings, thinking, "May all sentient beings throughout space and illustrated by my kind parents of this lifetime have happiness and the causes of happiness," then, even though there is only a little bit of help with respect to each sentient being and even though you meditate for only five minutes, because the scope is so vast, the virtue is inconceivable. If virtue had form, it would not fit in the whole world system. Virtue, however, is not physical, it is a product which is neither form nor consciousness. Virtues are latent predispositions which abide in the continuum of the mind.

Just as a little oil is taken from a single sesame seed, so with many it is possible to fill a pot with oil. In the same way, since sentient beings are limitless, if you meditate for the welfare of others, using this great field of awareness, wishing, "May all sentient beings have happiness and the causes of happiness," then the benefit from that one time is immeasurably great because it establishes very beneficial predispositions in the continuum of the mind.

Within our own country, do we not act lovingly toward our own children, our own friends? In just the same measure we are to act lovingly toward all sentient beings throughout all of space. Even if someone acts like an enemy toward us, we are to cultivate love toward him. We should cultivate love not only when someone acts well toward us, but when someone acts badly or in a middling manner toward us. To all of them we are one-pointedly, equally, to cultivate love.

The chief of all those activities you should assume is the cultivation of love—the wish that all sentient beings have happiness and the causes of happiness. This helps you in the future; in addition, you should do whatever should be done in your own country. To say, "I am doing religious practice", and not act in the service of your country is totally wrong.

Even if you are to die tomorrow or the day after tomorrow, you should meditate and study today.

Why is this? The Sakya Paṇḍita said that even if one is soon to die, one should learn the sciences, that though one will not become wise in this lifetime, one is certain to in his next birth. Thus, even if you are to die tomorrow, you should meditate, study and learn today.

There are many facets to meditation. You identify the causes of happiness, the ten virtues, the six perfections—giving, ethics, patience, effort, concentration and wisdom—and you then cultivate the wish that all sentient beings have these causes of happiness and happiness itself—live as gods and humans, resources, comfort and so forth.

In an actual session of practice you need to assume a meditative posture and set the mind one-pointedly without distraction on the object of meditation.

You should assume the sitting posture of the Buddha Vairocana, the adamantine (lotus) or the half (lotus) posture. Your eyes are not to look greatly upward nor are they to be shut, but are to be set evenly. If except for looking at the point of the nose you look to the right or the left, the mind will be distracted. Your backbone must be straight, without bending backward or forward or to the right or to the left. Your shoulders must be set straight without bending this way or that. Your head must be set naturally without being arched back or without being bent forward; your nose should be in line with your navel. Your lips and your teeth should be set naturally and freely, and your tongue should be put at the back of your upper teeth.

Your exhalation and inhalation of breath should not be noisy and should not be done with difficulty, but softly and gently. Allow the breath soundlessly and effortlessly to move in and out without purposefully making it slower or faster.

There are many different ways to place the hands, and you should do whatever suits you. There is one way with the hands on top of one another, the right hand on top of the left and placed in the center of the lap, called the position of meditative equipoise. There is one way where the left hand is placed flat on the lap with the palm upward and the right hand extends over the right knee touching the ground. This is called the posture of meditative equipoise touching the earth.

Another posture is like that of Avalokiteśvara, for the sake of resting; you set the palms of your hands flat on the ground at your sides. For those who are cramped, this is quite comfortable. In some postures, one holds as word or a book in his hands, but the posture of meditative equipoise is easier. If you are a little uncomfortable, sit in the posture of rest. It is very comfortable.

When it is time to meditate and your posture has been set correctly, considering one exhalation and one inhalation of breath as one unit, count your breaths until twenty-one. This will prevent your mind's being distracted elsewhere; it will prevent your ears hearing sounds, your eyes seeing forms, your nose smelling odors, your tongue perceiving tastes, your body feeling touches. These will not occur. The mind will thereby be set one-pointedly without distraction. Now you should call to mind your acquaintances of this lifetime and you should cultivate in meditation the thought, "May all sentient beings have happiness and the causes of happiness." This meditation is called the cultivation of love because you are being loving and beneficial towards all being.

Initially, this is not to be meditated too long, just for ten or fifteen minutes, then more and more by degrees. After you have meditated this way for months or years, you can make it longer and longer. It is not good to become completely tired.

Once you have cultivated the thought, "May all sentient beings possess happiness and the causes of happiness," and this meditation has been done for many, many years, then eventually you will attain what is called immeasurable love. When you have attained immeasurable love, you have meditative stabilization, meditative equipoise, and calm abiding.

You should leave aside a suitable length of time for meditation and cultivate love every day, continuously. You can meditate just before going to bed or early in the morning when you rise. If you cultivate love little by little, very clearly, then since the field of awareness is all sentient beings, sending love to all of them, it is as if you are repaying the immeasurable kindness which they extended to you in former lifetimes. When you meditate for the sake of the welfare of others, then your meditation is included within the activities of a being of greatest capacity from among the three types of beings: those of small, middling and great capacity.

Now let us break for a short period and when you return to meditate, assume the posture that I have described, begin the breathing exercise, and when about to meditate, call to mind your own father and mother of this lifetime, then make the aspiring prayer, "May all sentient beings throughout all of space, as illustrated by my own father and mother, have happiness and the causes of happiness." When you are about to leave the meditation you should dedicate it, thinking, "By the fruit of whatever virtue has arisen from the force of my hearing and thinking and meditating, may all beings be freed from cyclic existence and attain the rank of a perfect Buddha." Or, it is sufficient to say at the time of dedication, "May whatever virtue there is in having cultivated the thought, "May all sentient beings have happiness and the causes of happiness, help everyone throughout space."

What fault is there if you do not make a dedication? Even if you meditate well every day, when a little hatred arises, when someone pushes you and you immediately become angry, it is said that these virtues are destroyed. In the commentaries on Buddha's word it is said that the virtue accumulated over a thousand aeons is destroyed with one moment of anger.

When Śākyamuni Buddha was residing in Bodhgayā he told 2250 Hearers, "Anger destroys the roots of virtue." The Hearers thought, "If so, there is not one among us who does not get angry, thus none of our roots of virtue have remained. In the future none will remain. Even if we do virtue, it cannot be amassed." They were very worried; they thought, "If one moment of anger can destroy the virtues accumulated over a thousand aeons, then since we get angry many times every day, we do not have any virtue."

When they related this to Buddha, Buddha poured water into a little vessel and asked, "Will this water remain without evaporating?"

Because India is very hot, the Hearers thought, "In a few days the water will evaporate. This must mean that our virtue will not remain at all." They were extremely worried.

Then Buddha asked, "If this water is poured in the ocean, how long will it stay? It will remain until the ocean itself evaporates."

Therefore, if you do not just leave this virtue, but dedicate it, making a prayer petition that it become a cause of help and happiness for limitless sentient beings, then until that actually occurs, the virtue will not be lost. Like a small amount of water poured into the ocean, which will last until the ocean itself dries, so the fruit of your virtue will remain until it has ripened.

The benefit of hearing, thinking and meditating, in terms of causing all persons to possess happiness and the cause of happiness, is inconceivable. But if it is not dedicated, then when anger arises, it will be destroyed.

This benefit cannot be seen with the eye, but it is inconceivable. You are amazingly virtuous. I only think that it is wrong for me to sit above you. I should sit below you. It is wonderful that you feel to hear about this practice and meditate and cultivate it in meditation.

Now, rest a little and then when you return to meditate, sit as was explained before, count the breath for twenty-one inhalations and exhalations, meditate for about fifteen minutes and when it is time to stop, dedicate it as follows: "May whatever virtue there has been in my meditation and aspiration become a cause for happiness and comfort for all." Then you can rise and the meditation will be complete.

2
Compassion

ଔଷଡ

Chief within Buddhism is the practice of what is to be assumed and what is to be discarded. That which is to be assumed is happiness and that which is to be discarded is suffering. I have previously offered a little explanation about happiness, that which is to be assumed; now I will offer a little about that which is to be discarded.

Suffering is to be discarded. We must remove physical and mental discomfort from everyone, ourselves and others. Having identified the causes of suffering and the suffering that arises from those causes, we must make effort at the means to eradicate suffering. If we identify that such and such suffering arises from such and such cause, then both the causes and the effects will gradually be understood.

The causes of suffering are the ten non-virtues, the three physical non-virtues, the four verbal non-virtues, and the three mental non-virtues.

Among the three physical non-virtues, killing means to kill a human or any living being. There are three types of killing in terms of severity. The most severe is to kill your own father or mother or a Foe Destroyer. The effect of the most serious killing is to be born in a hell; of the middling, to be reborn as a hungry ghost; of the lesser, to be reborn as an animal. Killing only acts as the cause for undergoing variations of suffering, nothing else. In dependence on having killed, one is born in a bad migration. And then when one dies, even if one is reborn as a human, life will be very short. Because being born as a human is the effect of virtue and of maintaining ethics rather than an effect of killing, the necessity of a short life is due to the force of the fault of having killed in the past.

The second physical non-virtue is called taking what is not given. It means to steal or to overpower and rob. If you steal from another, through the force of that deed, in your future life you will have few resources, and whatever resources you have, others will steal. You will be left without anything, in a very difficult state.

The third physical non-virtue is called sexual misconduct. The worst form of sexual misconduct is for a father to copulate with his daughter or for a mother to copulate with her son. Therefore from the very beginning, among the religious systems of the world, there has been a prevalent prohibition against a father's copulating with his daughter or a mother's marrying her son, or brothers and sisters marrying. Sexual misconduct means to do these whereas they are not permitted.

Similarly, if one copulates in a church of whatever religion, or in front of an image which is an object of refuge, this is called sexual misconduct. If your wife is about to give birth to a child and you forcefully copulate with her, it is sexual misconduct. If you do such misconduct, in the future you will be controlled by desire and hatred.

Thus among the causes of suffering I have offered a brief identification of the three physical non-virtues, killing, stealing and sexual misconduct; there are more extensive explanations, but our purpose here is to give a brief identification.

There are four verbal non-virtues. The first is lying. It means to say that what is not or that what is not is, or that what one does not have one has, or that what one has, or does not have—to deceive. What will come from lying? In a future life no one will speak the truth to you; you will have the suffering of being filled with mistake and error.

The second verbal non-virtue is divisiveness. It means to stir people up by saying to someone, "He said such and such about you," when that person has not said it, and even to go to the other person and say, "So and so is blaming you." Such words, causing two people to disagree, are called divisive talk. The fruit of dividing people thus is that in a future life you will not have any friends; everyone will be disagreeable to you. Everything that others say to you will be an expression of fault about yourself. There will be no agreement.

The third verbal non-virtue is harsh speech. These are words rising anger in others, saying, "Stupid!", "Thief!", "Crazy!" and whatever comes to mind, to hurt. For instance, if it is necessary to tell someone to go here or there, you do not speak politely, "Go there," or "Come here," but say, "Can't you get over here?" "What are you doing? Aren't you going over there?" The effect of speaking harsh words is that in the future people will scold you. No matter what you say to others, others will only scold you. You will not find a chance to talk relaxed. You will be born in a place where you must always be scolded.

The fourth verbal non-virtue is senseless talk. This is to talk, not about religious practice, not about the affairs of your own family or the needs of your own friends, but to talk senselessly without any meaning at all. Not to talk about school, not about learning, not about technical training, but to waste your life unconscientiously. This is talk without accomplishing any purpose at all. Due to senseless talk people will not speak sense to you in a future birth; they will not say helpful good things. You will be purposeless, senseless, not knowing how to study; you will make noises from your mouth like a bird. You will be unable to sit still, unable to do effective work, unable to make good conversation, unable to write well—a destroyer of your own country and one who even further says, "Obeying the laws of the country is not right." You will say whatever comes to your mind, destroying systems of religious practice, destroying the laws of a country. You will be born in such a senseless state, talking gibberish.

Thus senseless talk is a cause of suffering. It is the cause for the appearance, in a future life, of the suffering of senselessness and confusion. No matter how much you would study, you could not possibly advance; you could not gain high rank or become a teacher, or be counted among the wise or be a secretary; you would have to be removed from the count of humans and cast into the count of animals.

I have explained the three physical and the four verbal causes which generate suffering. Now there are three mental causes of suffering. They are called covetousness, harmful intent, and wrong views.

Covetousness occurs when you have gone to a store or a market or see the property of another person, an attractive article, and you think, "I must definitely have that!" "How can I get that" "I must have this!" Then in the future you yourself will be poor and you will lose your own property to others.

Harmful intent occurs when you see someone, male, female, animal, no matter what, and think, "I will harm this one," "I will destroy this one," "I will make this one lower than I," or "I will cause this one to have a short life," or "I will destroy this one." This is harmful intent. Based on the force of it, in a future life no one will be good to you. When people see you, they will not like you. You will not have anyone at all in whom to place hope. There will be such great suffering.

The third mental non-virtue is called wrong views. The cause and effect of actions do exist, thus asserting that they do not exist is a wrong view. To hold that resources do not arise in the future from the giving of gifts, to hold that from miserliness you will not yourself become poor, to hold that from doing a virtuous cause there will be no happiness as its effect, to hold that from doing a non-virtue there will be no suffering or discomfort as its effect, to hold that from studying great qualities will not arise—that it only makes trouble and should be set aside—to hold that from killing you will not be born in a hell, these are wrong views.

In essence, wrong views mean that you perversely hold that if you do the three physical non-virtues or the four verbal non-virtues, there is no fault at all. When you engage in such wrong views, all the fruits of virtue which you previously had in your mental continuum are utterly destroyed. Because all roots of virtue have been utterly destroyed, there is the suffering of a lack of roots of virtue from giving; there is a lack of happiness of long life from forsaking killing. You are filled with such suffering.

The causes of suffering are the three physical non-virtues, the four verbal non-virtues, and the three mental non-virtues. At best you should not engage at all in the causes of suffering. If you do engage in them, do them only a little. If you have done them, then you should generate contrition.

Contrition, for example, is to feel that the physical non-virtues that you have done in the past are not at all suitable and to promise, "I will not do them in the future." By causing pain in your own mind with respect to these non-virtues, you cause their effects to become smaller. This affords great help to yourself.

Similarly, call to mind the four verbal non-virtues that you have done and think, "Those verbal non-virtues that I have done in the past are not at all suitable, and I will not do them in the future." The sins of the verbal non-virtues will become less, and you will bring great help to yourself; your suffering will lessen.

Then call to mind the three mental non-virtues that you have done and feel, "These mental non-virtues that I have done are not at all suitable and I will not do them in the future." Such virtuous contrition decreases the effects of the deeds and is a great boon.

At the conclusion of a contrite thought ask the Three Jewels for help to keep from doing these non-virtues in the future.

Although we say we do not want suffering, if we do not cease its causes, we will still generate suffering. Therefore we must make effort at freeing ourselves from suffering and the causes of suffering. If in making effort at this you hear, think and meditate only for your own sake, it has little meaning. However, if you make effort at the means of freeing all sentient beings, then the benefit is inconceivably great.

How do you engage in such meditation? Your field of intention is all sentient beings, and in order to accomplish the thought that they might attain liberation, you should make a petition to the Three Jewels, "O, Three Jewels—Buddha, Doctrine and Spiritual Community—I am cultivating the thought that all beings should become free of suffering and the causes of suffering. Please extend to me help in maturing the fruit of this meditation."

Within a petitioning state you should then do the meditation. You need first to identify the entities of suffering: birth, aging, sickness, death, hot, cold, hunger, and hatred. "May these and their causes, the ten non-virtues accumulated in my own and others' continuums, be totally extinguished."

The reason for the petition is that if you combine the strong force of your own thought and a strong object—the field of that thought—then the effect of the meditation will be accomplished quickly. In this case the strong force of thought is that you are contemplating freedom from suffering and the causes of suffering, the ten non-virtues, and are petitioning the Three Jewels. What is the strength of the object? If you take cognizance of all sentient beings—as illustrated by your own father and mother of this lifetime since they have been the kindest to you—the object itself has great strength. When these two are combined, the effect will quickly ripen. When you cultivate the prayer petition, "May all sentient beings, as illustrated by my father and mother of this lifetime, be free from suffering and the causes of suffering," you accumulate a great virtuous action.

There are four types of actions. If the force of the agent's own mind is strong and if the object—the field of intention—is special, then it becomes an action the effect of which is begun to be experienced in this very lifetime. If the meditation is not very strong, then it is called an action the effect of which is begun to be experienced in the next lifetime. If the force of the meditator's own thought is weak and the object itself is small, then it is the third type of action; its effect is begun to be experienced in the lifetime after the next lifetime. The beneficial effect does not come quickly. Further more, when you do not think about the field of intention and there is almost no force to your thought, and you just meditate, "May they be free from suffering and the causes of suffering," then this is called an uncertain action. It is not known when the effect will mature.

Thus, when initially meditating, go for refuge to the Three Jewels and think, "All beings should be freed from suffering and the causes of suffering; for the sake of this, I will meditate. May the intention of my meditation be achieved." When you take cognizance with great force of all sentient beings, the maturation of the effect will begin to take place right here in this lifetime.

When meditating assume the adamantine posture, or the half (lotus) posture. With regard to the mind, when you newly meditate, your mind may become scattered and there will be no possibility of meditation. Therefore, in order to stop the eye, ear, nose, tongue, and body consciousnesses and leave only the mental consciousness, you should count the breath. This is for the sake of stopping the senses. Some people, however, from the very beginning, are set to meditate. That which is to be meditated immediately appears to the mind; then it is fitting to meditate right away without counting the breath.

When you are about to leave the meditation, you should make a petition to the Three Jewels for help in order that whatever virtue has arisen from the session might become a cause of happiness for all sentient beings. Within such a petition, you should leave the meditation,

I have offered a little on these subjects today. If you have any questions, ask them.

Q. What are the Three Jewels?
A. The Three Jewels are the Buddha, his Doctrine, and the Spiritual Community. Buddha refers to the Buddhas themselves. Doctrine refers to the true cessations of the afflictions and the true paths leading to those cessations. The Spiritual Community are the Hearer Superiors, Solitary Realizer Superiors, and Bodhisattva Superiors. These are the actual refuge. The similitudes of refuge are an image of Buddha, books of his teaching, and the Spiritual Community of monks and nuns. An image of a Buddha is not the actual Buddha, and monks and nuns are not actual Hearer, Solitary Realizer, or Bodhisattva Superiors. However, these can serve the function of the Three Jewels, and through them your purpose can be achieved.

Q. When we cultivate the thought, "May all sentient beings be free from suffering and the causes of suffering," what are we to think?

A. You are to think, "May they be separated from the sufferings which are to be born, grow old, become sick, and die through the power of tainted actions and affliction—to become hungry, thirsty, to undergo what one does not want, to suffer heat and cold." You need to think that if in the future they are born in a bad migration, they will have the immeasurable suffering of a hell being, a hungry ghost or an animal. Even if they are not born in a bad migration but are born as a god or a human, still there is great suffering through the force of tainted actions and afflictions—birth, old age, sickness, and death. You are developing the aspiration that they be free from pain.

Q. When you count your breath and become distracted, what should you do?

A. You may either go back and begin counting again from one, or begin again at the number where you became distracted.

3
JOY
ের০

In the Buddhist system of religious practice, persons are identified from the point of view of their capacity. They are called beings of great, middling, and small capacity. Among these three types of beings, the beings of small capacity are also divided into three; small of the small, middling of the small and great of the small.

The small of the small are those who strive after the happiness of this life, and except for that, they do not think about anything. They do not engage in the practice of Buddhism, Christianity, Islam, and so forth. As an example of such a being there are cows, or even if they are human, they only destroy religious practice; they do not achieve any virtue at all. They are like animals.

The middling of the small engage in both religious and non-religious practices. The intent of their practice is to achieve only the happiness of this life. Even though they do engage in religious practice, it is not for the sake of their parents or of their future lives, but only for the sake of happiness in this lifetime itself. The way in which a being whose capacity is middling of the small engages in his so-called religious practice is not suitable; therefore, it actually cannot function as religious practice.

The great of the small, or the best of the small, mainly engage in religious practice for the sake of their future lives. They do indeed seek happiness, comfort, food, drink, resources and so forth for this lifetime, but this is not their main activity. They are mainly seeking happiness in future lives. Such seekers are called beings whose capacity is the best of the small. The religious practice done by such persons is not for the sake of others. It is for their own welfare. Among actual religious practitioners, those who are engaged in religious practice for the sake of achieving happiness within cyclic existence in a future lifetime are the lowest of the low.

Why are they seeking happiness in future lives? They have

identified the cause and effect of actions and they know their sins and virtues. They know that after death they will experience pleasures in their future lives from virtuous causes and that they will experience sufferings due to non-virtuous causes. They know that this life will finish and that when it does finish, if in their future lives they are born in bad migrations as hell beings, hungry ghosts, or animals, they will have great suffering. They know that if they are born as gods or humans, it will be a little better. Therefore they seek a good migration in the future. They know that no matter how long this lifetime is, it will not last many years and that there are innumerable births in future lives until cyclic existence is finished. Therefore, rather than seek their own welfare in this lifetime, which is so short, and suffer for it in the future in a bad migration, they begin to engage in religious practice.

Initially, in their religious practice they go for refuge. They go for refuge with great strength because their refuge is preceded by two causes: they have concern for their own sufferings in bad migrations and believe that the Three Jewels have the power to protect them from those sufferings. Therefore, they go for refuge from the depths of their hearts to the Three Jewels, relying on the Three Jewels, asking for their protection and help.

If when you begin to go for refuge these two causes are merely mouthed or are only words, then even though you go for refuge, that refuge will only be mouthed and only be words. But if the two causes of refuge, concern over your own sufferings in bad migrations and the belief that the Three Jewels have the power to protect you from these sufferings, are thoroughly believed—in the sense of a thorough discrimination—then the two causes which precede refuge will be actual and the refuge itself will be real.

When you go for refuge, you should set in your mind these two causes for refuge and then say, "I go for refuge to the Lama, I go for refuge to the Buddha, I go for refuge to the Doctrine, I go for refuge to the Spiritual Community."

The Three Jewels are Buddha, Doctrine, and Spiritual Community. I will tell you the history behind putting, "I go for refuge to the Lama" first.

When Buddha was about to die in his eighty-first year, he informed his students, "I am about to die." Mañjughoṣa and Vajrapāṇi asked him, "When you die, whom can we ask about the doctrine? On whom can we rely? It is very difficult looking at the external shape of a person; we will not know what is best for us to do."

The teacher Buddha said, "If in the future you request to be taught doctrine, I will bless and enter the form of your Lama (guru in Sanskrit). If you have faith that he is I, this will act as faith in me." Since that time, when refuge is taken, we have said, "I go for refuge to the Lama, I go for refuge to the Buddha, I go for refuge to the Doctrine, I go for refuge to the Spiritual Community." Still, there are not four jewels; there are only three.

Saying refuge is merely words. The actual meaning is that from within the depths of your own mind you are relying on the Lama, Buddha, Doctrine and Spiritual Community, in the sense of asking them for help. Doing this with a mind of reliance and firm faith and having strong discrimination which is mindful of the qualities of Buddha, Doctrine, and Spiritual Community, you have real refuge. Thus, there are two types of refuge: verbal and actual.

Whether a person has refuge or not is determined by four qualities: whether the person knows the attributes of the Three Jewels, knows their differences and accepts them as the pure source of refuge—the latter means that one accepts that there is no greater place of refuge than the Three Jewels—and will not propound any other source of refuge. If understanding of these has formed in your mind, then even if you are sleeping, awake or working or studying, it can function as continuously having refuge.

If you are among the best of the small who have great intelligence, you have much to think about at this point. You think, "For the sake of not being born in a bad migration in my future life—as a hell being or hungry ghost or an animal—and for the sake of being born in a good migration—as a god or a human—I am going for refuge to the Three Jewels." Then you wonder, "Is that sufficient?" When you examine this, you see that even if you ask the Three Jewels for help in attaining the rank of a god or a human in your next lifetime, and even if you attain the rank of a god or a human in your next lifetime, you will be born, grow old, become sick, and die. Therefore, merely gaining happiness in the next lifetime is not sufficient. You have arrived at great understanding.

Whether a life is good or bad, unless you do not have to take rebirth at all through the force of contaminated actions, it is not at all suitable. When such understanding forms, you have exceeded the qualities of thought of beings of small capacity. But still you have not arrived at the state of the middling or great but you are superior to the small.

Progressing in your thought, you gradually decide that you must obtain liberation from all types of cyclic existence and no longer be subject to birth by the force of contaminated actions and afflictions; you must have the bliss of the extinguishment of suffering. You realize that the cause of contaminated actions is the afflictions themselves and that this enemy causes the trouble.

Thus you think, "Having overcome this enemy which is the afflictions, I must attain freedom from bondage. I must attain happiness which is the extinguishment of all suffering for myself." This thought to gain liberation from cyclic existence is the attitude of a being of middling capacity.

Your refuge then also has two causes. You have concern for your own suffering and you believe that the Three Jewels have the power to protect you. Because you are then acting solely for your own welfare and not seeking the welfare of others, you have not become a being of great capacity. As one of middling capacity, you petition the Three Jewels, and through engaging in the proper meditation you can liberate yourself from cyclic existence.

When, having concern for your own suffering and believing that the Three Jewels have the power to protect you, you go for refuge from the depths of your heart, you have a pure form of refuge, no matter whether you are meditating or working. Engaging in the proper practices for a being of middling capacity, you can become either a Hearer Foe Destroyer or a Solitary Realizer Foe Destroyer, able to remain in a pleasant state. No benefit at all is gained for others—your own father and mother. You are acting for your own welfare, and thus do not exceed middling religious practice. I will later offer an extensive explanation of how such a person not only does not bring about the welfare of others, but also does not fulfill his own aims. Thus I have explained the mode of thought of one who, seeking his own welfare, passes from the best of the small to the middling capacity.

Now I will explain the history of a being of superior mental force who passes from the capacity of the great of the small to the greatest capacity. You think, "Even though I attain the happiness of a god or a human in the next lifetime; I will still die; happiness in the next lifetime is not sufficient." But, not seeking your own welfare alone, you think about all sentient beings, "It is not sufficient for all sentient beings, as illustrated by my father and mother, just to attain happiness in their next lifetime. Unless they all become freed from cyclic existence, it will not help for them merely not to be born in a bad migration in their next lifetime and to attain a happy migration, because at the end of that, they will die and be reborn. Therefore, not just myself but everyone should be liberated from bondage." You are then on your way to developing the greatest capacity directly from the stage of the best of the small.

There are two causes that generate your refuge: you have concern for four faults in sentient beings—their cyclic existence, their seeking solitary peace which is mere liberation for their own sake, their obstructions to liberation, and their obstruction, to omniscience. You believe that the Three Jewels have the power to protect all from these four faults, and you go for refuge to the Three Jewels from the depths of your heart. When you become a being of greatest capacity, you forsake your own welfare and are intent upon the welfare of others.

Although you have forsaken your own welfare, your own welfare is accomplished as it could not be in any other way. As an example of this, if the head of a country forsakes his own welfare and is intent upon the welfare of others, his own country benefits greatly. In seeking peace for the world itself, even though he has forsaken his own welfare and is intent upon the welfare of others, he himself becomes famous and everyone respects him. Even when he dies, everyone thinks, "Oh, there was such and such a person!" "Oh, there used to be such and such a person!" Just as he is respected not only by his own people but also by the people of other countries, so in terms of religious practice, when you forsake your own welfare and are intent on establishing others in happiness, happiness spontaneously arises along the way, even though you make no effort in your own behalf.

Thus, there are three types of refuge, as performed by the best of the small, the middling, and the great. If we can actually do it, we should engage in the refuge of a being of greatest capacity. One instance of refuge by the great is more powerful than one hundred thousand refuges by the small. Whether you are hearing, thinking, or meditating, you should precede such practice with refuge.

Thus with regard to our refuge today we should petition the Three Jewels, "I am concerned about all sentient beings. I am concerned about their cyclic existence, solitary peace and two obstructions, and I believe that the Three Jewels have the power to protect all sentient beings from these faults. I am asking the Three Jewels from the depth of my heart for help. For the sake of that, I will meditate. Please aid me in making it successful."

There are discussions about the unsuitability of solitary peace and there are seven cause and effect precepts to aid a being whose capacity is the best of the small to become of great capacity. If I explained them to you today, I could not finish. May I explain them to you later? Now I will explain today's meditation.

Once you have taken refuge, the meditation is to cultivate the thought of joy, "May all sentient beings not be separate from a happiness free from suffering." Why do we cultivate this? Usually, even when you have happiness and good resources such as food and drink, clothing, and a place to live, you still must suffer sickness, hot, cold, danger, fighting, and so forth. There is mental and physical discomfort. Even when you have happiness, it actually is not just happiness; it is mixed with suffering like food that is mixed with poison. Our situation is very difficult.

What exactly is the meditation? It is to petition the Three Jewels and ask for help that all sentient beings—as illustrated by our own parents of this lifetime—have only happiness, that they not be separated from a happiness free of suffering, that they have the physical and mental attributes of a life of high status, and that they all ultimately have the bliss of liberation from cyclic existence.

Our sessions here are fifteen minutes, but in your own home a shorter, clear session is better—for five or ten minutes. Then when you are about to leave the meditation, petition the Three Jewels thinking, "May whatever benefit that has arisen from this meditation fructify for all sentient beings throughout all of space." Press your palms together with the thumbs between the palms.

Your intention to take refuge and to meditate has great merit, and it is difficult to find such people in the world. Not even considering doing this continuously, there are stories of quickly becoming a Buddha through establishing predisposing tendencies from a single such meditative session.

When you meditate, first go for refuge to the Three Jewels from the depths of your heart with concern for the frights of cyclic existence, solitary peace and the two obstructions in all sentient beings and with belief that the Three Jewels have the power to protect beings from these four. Then after meditation, make a petition that the merit of the session, the benefit of the session, go to help all sentient beings. If you have any questions, please ask them.

Q.   When we petition this way, what power do the Three Jewels have?

A.   Buddha is the revealer of refuge, the Doctrine is the actual refuge, and the Spiritual Community are the helpmates for achieving refuge. Since the Doctrine is the actual refuge, we need to identify it clearly. The Buddha's Doctrines are the scriptures—of which there are three divisions—and the paths—of which there are the three trainings.

Scriptures which mainly teach training in higher ethics are the division of discipline. Scriptures which mainly teach training in higher meditative stabilization are the division of discourses. Scriptures which mainly teach training in higher wisdom are the division of knowledge.

With regard to the paths, there are three trainings: ethics, meditative stabilization, and wisdom. Ethics are of three types: individual liberation, Bodhisattva, and secret mantra. Even if you keep the lowest of these vows, the vows of individual liberation, you will be reborn in a good migration, taking rebirth in a life of high status as a god or a human. As Candrakīrti says in his Supplement, "Other than ethics, there is no cause of high status."

When you cultivate the training in higher meditative stabilization, you attain clairvoyances: of eye, of ear, remembering other lifetimes, knowing other persons' minds, and magical emanation. Ultimately you can liberate yourself from bondage. Similarly, when you generate the training in higher wisdom, you generate the wisdom directly cognizing the ultimate truth, emptiness. When that is generated, you can attain the final truth of the three vehicles, their respective paths of no more learning. All of these are caused by training in higher wisdom.

Therefore, when you take refuge, you are taking refuge in Buddha—the revealer of refuge, in the Doctrine—the actual refuge, and in the Spiritual Community—your helpers to achieving refuge. Thus when you can practice actual refuge, do what is to be done, and discard what is not to be done, you finally are liberated. Such a system of religious practice appears only in a place where people have great merit. In other places it will not increase, it will disappear.

Q.   If a person makes great effort for the sake of others but does not engage in religious practice, of what capacity is he said to be?

A.   Except that he says from his mouth that he is not engaging in religious practice, he accords with the ways of religious practice, thus there is great benefit. If it is for the sake of his own fame, however, there is no benefit. If he does not think about fame for himself and seeks to remove faults from others then his activity is motivated by compassion.

Q.   Among the four faults, cyclic existence, solitary peace, and the two obstructions, what is wrong with peace?

A.   This peace is an extinguishment of suffering only for one's own sake. When you are freed from cyclic existence and have attained the state of a Foe Destroyer, you do not need resources, food, and clothing, nor do you need to sleep. You are not reborn and do not become old, sick, and die. You can stay in trance for even a thousand aeons and it seems only like an hour. However, you are not at all helping other sentient beings and are far from achieving Buddhahood.

The Buddhas then rouse a Foe Destroyer saying, "Not even considering the welfare of others, even though you do not have to wander in cyclic existence, you have not perfected your own welfare. Rise from your meditative stabilization and enter into the Mahāyāna as a being of greatest capacity." Exhorted by the Buddhas' speech, they rise from meditative stabilization.

There are cases in India and in Tibet, in mountain cave retreats, where those who have spent an aeon in meditative stabilization have finally left their bodies. While they were meditating, their fingernails wrapped around their bodies many times. Their corpse, with their fingernails encircling it, is all that is left for us to see, after the Buddhas have caused them to rise. I have seen five or six in India and only two in Tibet. Such practice is a protracted path. One who passes from the level of the best of the small and becomes a being of great capacity has already finished attaining Buddhahood, while this one, who passed on only to the middling type of being, is remaining in meditative stabilization.

Thus, in the beginning, practicing is much better than not. Then, engaging in the practices of a being of middling capacity is better than engaging in the practices of the best of the small. However, this is not the most complete form of practice because such a person has not even fulfilled his own welfare, never mind the welfare of others. Therefore, he is said to be abiding only in a solitary peace, and to be in trouble.

4
Equanimity
ↄ⌘ↄ

Previously in our meditation we cultivated the thought, "May all sentient beings have happiness," then, "May all sentient beings be free from suffering," then, "May all sentient beings not be separate from a happiness free of suffering." Therefore, today our meditation is concerned with cultivation of the wish that persons might be free of intimacy and alienness or desire and hatred.

Through the power of intimacy and alienness, some persons are objects of great friendliness, and others are objects of hatred and complete unsuitability. If you engage in these, it is unsuitable for yourself and also for your country. Each and every one of us has intimacy and alienness, desire and hatred, until we become Bodhisattvas. Let us identify them.

Let us use an example that each of us knows: When someone who is friendly with us dies, we are very worried and cry; it is difficult for us. We feel, "Oh, this person died. How awful it is!" This is because the person was very close to us, was desirable. In terms of the worry you undergo when such a person is sick, it is just as if you yourself were sick.

Someone who is not on friendly terms with us is said to be distant. A sign of this distance, or alienness, is that if this person dies, we are happy. We say, "Oh, that is fine," and take pleasure in his death. When someone who is neither very close through desire nor an enemy through hatred dies, we just feel, "Oh," and leave the matter. We do not even have the worry we would have if one of our own cups broke. When a person is close and involved in desire, we worry as if we ourselves were sick; when a distant person, an alien, is sick and dies, we take pleasure in it. This is called intimacy and alienness.

Because this world is a place of cyclic existence, there is desire and hatred. If you do not abide in equanimity, free from these, then in the world some will be friendly, and to them you in turn will be friendly; toward those who are unfriendly you will have the wish to fight and kill, and if you cannot kill them, you will act badly toward them. If you do not have a sense of equanimity, believing that all living beings—hell beings, hungry ghosts, animals, humans, demigods and gods—should equally have happiness and should equally be free of suffering, then pure religious practice and pure meditation cannot take place.

In order to gain such an equanimity, we engage in meditation; we reflect on the fact that all living beings, even though they are not our parents in this lifetime, were our parents in former births. What is the fault if we do not know this?

The present Dalai Lama is the sixty-seventh incarnation of Avalokiteśvara, who has been appearing in the world since the time of Śākyamuni Buddha to help sentient beings. Among those sixty-seven there were seven adepts with clairvoyance, abiding in meditative equipoise. One of them was wandering about the world to see what forms of intimacy and alienness were present in the world, and whether people were agreeing or disagreeing. There are five clairvoyances: With the divine eye one can see whatever is occurring presently in the one billion worlds of this world system. With the divine ear, one can hear whatever is said in the one billion worlds of this world system as if people were speaking right nearby. With the clairvoyance of knowing one's own and others' rebirths one can know, for many aeons and for each person, how and where they were born and whatever they did. With the clairvoyance of knowing others' minds, one can know what other sentient beings are thinking. With the clairvoyance of magical creations one can fly in the air, pass through walls and so forth. If you meditate, you can attain these.

Now, he had such clairvoyance, and as he approached a family he saw a young woman who was cudding her child on her lap. The mother loved her child. She was sitting there eating the flesh of a lamb. She set the meat next to her; a dog came and took away the meat. The mother threw a stone at the dog, almost killing him. When the adept looked with his clairvoyance, he saw that the mother's parents had an enemy who destroyed their household. He died and took rebirth as the child the woman held, and she was being very friendly with him, her family's enemy. The mother's father had died and taken rebirth as a sheep; she was eating the flesh of the sheep, her father. Her mother had died and had taken rebirth as a dog, and she had thrown a stone, almost killing the dog, her mother.

The adept was saddened and sorrowfully thought, "She cuddles on her lap the enemy who destroyed her family, she eats the flesh of her father, and she throws a stone at the head of her mother and almost kills her," and he wept.

Thus all sentient beings have been your own parents in the past; it is only through the fault of desire and hatred that we think some are suitable and friendly toward them and we think that others are not suitable and act badly toward them. Nothing good will come of it. How is this?

Through the force of desire toward the intimate, the close, we generate attachment, liking these people very much, and toward the distant we become angry. But in former lives all these persons, both the intimate and the alien, have been our enemies or our friends. Those with whom we are so friendly now as children, family members, our own parents—these persons were our enemies in a former life. There is not one who has not been our enemy. How are you to meditate on this?

You are to think that there is not any among all the various sentient beings throughout all of space who has not been your parent. This is said in Buddha's scriptures; it is also the way things are.

Cyclic existence is beginningless. Thus, there is not any sentient being who has not nurtured you. Just as your own parents in this lifetime have been kind, so all other sentient beings in former lifetimes have extended just as great kindness to you. Thus, you should recognize all sentient beings as your mother in a former lifetime and has been as kind to you as your mother of this lifetime. If someone is acting like an enemy toward you, then you should think that because this person sustained you in a former lifetime, "I will not answer with anger and fight, but will recognize him as my mother."

So the first step in the meditation is the recognition of all sentient beings as your mother. The second is to be mindful of their kindness; this means that when you see another person, even though do not know when he was your mother, you think, "At some time this person was as kind to me as my own parents in this lifetime." Even if he is angry with you, you feel, "I will not answer this anger. He was very kind to me in the past." Thus you should be mindful of the kindness of sentient beings.

The third step in the meditation is the intent to repay the kindness. You have become mindful of their great kindness in that initially your body formed in their womb, and when you were born, each took care of you until you finished school. Their sustenance was like taking out a loan, and if you do not repay it, then due to that, you will undergo much suffering. Thus the third step is to think, "I will repay their kindness."

The fourth step is a love in the sense of pleasantness. This means that even though living beings, hell denizens, hungry ghosts, animals—including bugs, birds, and cats—and human beings and so forth, might not be your parents right now, they have been very kind in the past. Even if now they are your enemies, in a previous birth they were your friends and thus are all equally pleasant to you, and you want all of them to have happiness and comfort. Even though some are now acting like enemies, you should think, "They should have happiness. Those that I recognize as parents and those that I do not recognize as parents are the same. All of them should have comfort and happiness."

This is a love in the sense of pleasantness. When you cultivate love, you think, "Even though this one might be harming me now, this person was a parent in the past, and even though that other one might be friendly to me now, that person was an enemy in the past, and thus they are both the same. Even if someone scolds me I should cultivate patience; I should not answer him in kind, I should not fight."

If patience is not cultivated in meditation, as soon as someone says harsh words, as soon as someone just bumps into you, you will begin to fight. When our minds become worse and worse—not even considering the religious practice of overcoming intimacy and alienness—we are angry for a long time, and that anger destroys roots of virtue created before. Thus if you do not cultivate patience, there is great fault.

In the past, in the eastern part of India, there was a religious practitioner who went to his guru to receive precepts. He was told to cultivate in meditation a pleasant love and patience. He did so and when he left his meditation and went outside, someone said a rough word to him, and the practitioner answered bitterly and hit him. Others criticized him, saying that he was not a practitioner, that he had not meditated well, and that hatred had arisen in him. They said, "Your cultivation of patience was not complete." He laughed and said that he would perform a meditation which would exceed anything that any of them could do.

He went back to his room and stayed without going outside. A friend thought that he might have overly criticized him for his poor meditation, and now that he was meditating well, he would test him to see if his friend actually could cultivate patience in meditation. So he defecated on a plate and carrying that plate with him, went to the practitioner's room and asked, "What are you doing?"

The meditator said, "I am cultivating patience. I am cultivating patience."

His friend asked, "What kind of patience are you cultivating?"

"I am cultivating a patience such that no matter what anyone says, no matter how anyone is, I will not answer him back."

So his friend said, "If you have patience and will not answer anyone back, then, eat shit," and put the plate in front of the meditator.

The meditator immediately picked up the plate, threw it at his friend, and said, "You eat shit!"

His friend picked up the plate and left, saying, "You are not cultivating patience." Then the meditator was sad. He thought, "Oh, I really am not cultivating patience. My friend did not get angry. He did not answer back. He must have been testing me to see if I was successful, and when I threw the plate at him, he did not get angry. He is not without patience, but when he set it near me, I got angry. He must have been testing to see whether I had attained patience or not." Thus he was contrite and understood that he himself was at fault. He meditated with great effort and succeeded. To prevent such occurrences, he cultivated pleasant love, first recognizing sentient beings as mothers, then recognizing their kindness, then developing the intent to repay their kindness.

When you feel that you should repay people's kindness, then no matter what they do to you, they are all good, everyone is good. This is called a love in the sense of pleasantness, a love wherein all sentient beings are pleasant to you. When love has been cultivated, then there is compassion.

Toward all beings throughout space—humans, bugs, everyone— you now have equanimity, which is freedom from desire and hatred. You consider everyone equally and wish that they might all be free of suffering. This is called compassion. The thought is, "All sentient beings must be free of suffering." If you do not think that all sentient beings are the same in wanting happiness and not wanting suffering, then you do not have equanimity—freedom from intimacy, alienness, desire and hatred—and it is very difficult to develop great compassion and great love. You could, perhaps, have a little compassion and a little love, but not great compassion and great love. Why is it difficult?

Just as when that meditator was meditating and his friend came and told him to eat shit and he immediately became angered, if you do not cultivate equanimity, then love and compassion are impossible. Toward those people who do not praise you, you will even generate a wish that they have suffering. Therefore practice compassion.

The sixth step is the unusual attitude. What is this?

It is not just to have the aspiration of love that all sentient beings have happiness. It is for you to take up the burden yourself to cause them to become happy. "I will make them happy." This thought is the unusual attitude of love. "I will cause all to be free of suffering and the causes of suffering." This is the unusual attitude of compassion.

When you have completely developed the thought in meditation, "I myself will cause all sentient beings to possess happiness and to become free of suffering," then you have become a being of greatest capacity. You voluntarily take up the burden to free all from suffering and the causes of happiness. And then, when you continue to meditate with great force, you think, "Even though I have taken on this burden, there are innumerable sentient beings, equal to the limits of space, going from the hells on up; although I will help all these, I cannot do it now. Why? How could I separate them from suffering when I cannot even free myself from suffering? Thus in order to do this, I will attain the rank of a Buddha and will draw them all up to Buddhahood. Other than that, I am afflicted and cannot pull them up out of suffering."

Thinking this, you generate an altruistic aspiration to highest enlightenment, "I will attain the position of a completely perfect Buddha for the sake of being able to cause all sentient beings to have happiness and to become free of suffering."

When this thought is completely generated and spontaneously exists in your mental continuum, you have generated bodhicitta, an altruistic mind of enlightenment. You have generated the first level of the Mahāyāna path of accumulation. You are now a Mahāyānist, a Bodhisattva. Thus the generation of an aspiration to highest enlightenment for the sake of all sentient beings is the door of the Mahāyāna, just as refuge is the door to the proper practice of Buddhism. In order to generate an altruistic mind of enlightenment the seven-fold cause and effect precepts are taught: recognition of all sentient beings as mothers, mindfulness of their kindness, intent to repay their kindness, pleasant love, compassion, an unusual attitude, and the actual generation of an altruistic aspiration to highest enlightenment itself.

Today I have told you a little about the seven-fold cause and effect precepts. In our three previous meditations we cultivated the thought, "May all have happiness and the causes of happiness, may all be free of suffering and the causes of suffering, and may all not be separate from a happiness free of suffering." Now the fourth is: "May all sentient beings abide in an equanimity free from intimacy and alienness, desire and hatred. May they not fight, sometimes considering others to be alien and sometimes considering others to be intimate. May they abide valuing everyone equally." This is our meditation for today.

Through merely cultivating this thought in meditation, all sentient beings will not come to have happiness, nor will they lose their suffering; still we can cease the sense of alienness and intimacy, desire and hatred in our own continuum.

Through our cultivating in meditation the thought, "May all sentient beings have happiness and the causes of happiness," they will not become happy, but because they were all extremely kind to us in the past, the benefit of repaying that debt is of immeasurable virtue. In the same way, when we cultivate in meditation the thought, "May all sentient beings be free of suffering and the causes of suffering"—even though they do not by this all become free of suffering—there is tremendous benefit for both oneself and others because this helps one's own mental continuum. Our meditations to date of love, compassion, joy, and now equanimity are in general helpful in that they are the substantive causes for attaining Buddhahood.

Today, when you meditate, cultivate the thought, "May all sentient beings—as illustrated by my father and mother of this lifetime—abide in equanimity free of alienness and intimacy, desire and hatred, no longer desirously attached too much to the intimate, fighting with the alien, killing them, or thinking that they should kill them. May they abide in equanimity valuing all the same, liking all the same."

If this meditation is done strongly, in the end there will be peace without war in the world; even if the meditation is not done very strongly, still there will be the immediate benefit that in our future lives you will not meet with angrisome persons and people will like you. When you take birth in a future life as a human or an animal, others will respect you, will not be angry, will not be overly attached; nor will they be hateful; they will be even-minded toward you.

Thus, assume the adamantine posture as explained previously, and if your mind is distracted, then count your breath until twenty-one for the sake of stopping your sense consciousnesses. If that is not needed, then it is suitable to mediate immediately. Take refuge, "I go for refuge to the Lama, I go for refuge to the Buddha, I go for refuge to the Doctrine, I go for refuge to the Spiritual Community." Then cultivate the thought, "May all sentient beings abide in an equanimity free of intimacy and alienness, desire and hatred." When the meditation is finished, dedicate the merit to all beings: "May all beneficial virtues of having meditated today go as the cause of all sentient beings' abiding in equanimity."

I have explained this in brief. If you have any questions, please ask them.

Q. When one goes for refuge to the Three Jewels, how do they help?
A. If you ask for help for the sake of all sentient beings, then special help is given. When you ask for help for your own sake, not very much help is afforded, but when your motivation is altruistic, then empowerment immediately comes. The Three Jewels are unlike anything else. When you ask for help, the Three Jewels know of your request. How is this? Of the Three Jewels, Buddha and the Spiritual Community are engaged only in the welfare of all sentient beings throughout all space. When someone asks for help they are pleased and immediately give such help.

Q. Are we to meditate on the seven cause and effect precepts today?
A. If you are able now to cultivate these seven cause and effect precepts in meditation, that is fine. Even your intention to do so is good. Still, the meditation today is equanimity. We are cultivating equanimity in order to be able to achieve the seven cause and effect precepts. The cause for entering the path of the Mahāyāna is an altruistic mind generation; the means to do this are the seven cause and effect precepts. They were passed from Śākyamuni Buddha to the protector Maitreya through Asaṅga on down to us here today. There is another system, called the switching of self and other, which was transmitted from Śākyamuni Buddha to Mañjughoṣa and down through the ages to us today.

Even if you do not practice the seven cause and effect precepts in meditation but merely think about them, the benefit is incomparable. You will understand this in the future.

5

Cyclic Existence

❧

I will offer you the reasons for designating the name, 'path' to
practices in the Buddhist system. What is a path? Through causing
one to discard what is to be discarded and to adopt what is to be
adopted, these practices lead one by stages to the rank of a Buddha
or of a Foe Destroyer. Therefore, like a road which is a place of travel,
these practices are called paths.

There are many types of paths that lead to Buddhahood or to the
state of a Foe Destroyer, the paths of Hearers, the paths of Solitary
Realizers, and the paths of Bodhisattvas. However, among all these,
the best of them are the three principal paths: the intention definitely
to leave cyclic existence, the aspiration to highest enlightenment for
the sake of all sentient beings, and the correct view of emptiness.

The intention to leave cyclic existence is the path of the thought
either for oneself, or for oneself and all other sentient beings, definitely
to gain freedom from bondage.

What does it mean to leave cyclic existence? Cyclic existence is a
state of being moved by the force of contaminated actions and
afflictions to assume contaminated mental and physical aggregates,
and then once these aggregates have been assumed, to be born, grow
old, become sick, and die, stage by stage, in the six types of migrations.

Why are we travelling in cyclic existence? The causes are
contaminated actions and afflictions. The afflictions are the six root
afflictions and the twenty secondary afflictions, but among them the
chief are desire, hatred, and ignorance. These are called the three
poisons. Except for Hearer, Solitary Realizer, and Bodhisattva
Superiors, there are none among us who do not accumulate actions
by the force of desire, hatred, and ignorance. Ourselves and all other
common beings powerlessly engage in actions through these three,
desire, hatred, and ignorance.

Through desire we accumulate various actions due to liking food, drink, and resources. For example, due to liking an article too much, we might steal it, or we might do something that is not permitted, or engage in lust through many forms of desire.

Through hatred we fight, kill, and fall into disrepute. Obscured through ignorance, not knowing that we will be involved in non-virtue, we powerlessly accumulate sin. Through the force of desire, hatred, ignorance, and other afflictions, we accumulate actions. Even if we do not wish to do so, due to the force of our own conditioning over beginningless aeons, we continuously accumulate such actions. If we amass great non-virtue, we are born in the hells, if we amass middling non-virtue, we are born as animals. Thus through three different measures of non-virtue we are born in other lifetimes in bad migrations. If we amass virtuous actions, we are born as gods, demi-gods and humans.

With respect to being born in the hells through accumulating great non-virtues, there are eight hot hells, eight cold hells, trifling hells, and neighboring hells. Among these I will offer just one example of rebirth in the first of the eight hot hells, called Reviving.

When we are born in the Reviving Hell, due to our former actions, we immediately have weapons in our hands and are powerlessly fighting each other—cutting up each other until we all fall down unconscious. Then from the sky a voice issues, saying, "Revive!" We revive, and our bodies are again as they were when we were first born there, because in the hells we do not die, no matter how much we are mutilated, until our lifespan is exhausted. Again, we rise and having been healed, fight a hundred thousand times, cutting each other to pieces, falling down unconscious, reviving, and so forth. Until our life span is exhausted there is no chance to enjoy, to be comfortable, to stay by one's self. There is not even an hour's interruption.

When we are born in the hells, even if we do not usually have clairvoyance, we have memory of our former life. When first born in a hell we know that in a former lifetime we were born as a god or a human, but that we accumulated such and such a bad action and due to that cause we must now suffer. This clairvoyance is not due to having formerly cultivated meditative stabilization. Through the force of our own actions, we know our past life for a short while, as if seeing it with our own eyes, and then we no longer remember. This clairvoyance, which is not due to the power of meditation, also occurs in the six types of desire gods—the Four Great Royal Lineages, the Heaven of the Thirty-Three, the Without Combat, the Joyous, the Liking Emanation, and the Controlling Others' Emanation. These six types of gods usually enjoy the desirous resources of pleasant form, pleasant sound, pleasant odor, pleasant taste, and pleasant touch. Unlike humans and animals, the desire gods are very comfortable. They are born like hell beings, not from a womb, but spontaneously. As soon as we are born in a hell, we undergo suffering. In the same way, as soon as we are born as a god, we enjoy pleasures. The gods live immeasurable life spans and though we live comfortably, during the seven days preceding our death, we realize that we are going to die. The light of our body fades, our garlands wilt, and we begin to smell. The other gods, realizing that we are about to die, no longer offer flowers and no longer come nearby. We undergo such suffering.

While we suffer over these seven days we know that we will die from that place and be born as a hell being, hungry ghost, or animal and see our birthplace as if with our own eyes. We know that we will undergo such and such suffering; we are very disturbed.

Among the six types of desire gods, the lowest are the Four Lineages of Great Kings. Fifty years in our world are one day in their world; therefore their seven days of discomfort are three hundred fifty of our years. Through the force of their own great comfort, they do not reveal, confess, and overcome the sins which they accumulated formerly, and finally knowing what they must undergo due to their former bad actions, they suffer miserably; like hell beings they have clairvoyance not from meditation but due to their former actions, and they are mentally pained by the misery they see that they will undergo.

Now let us consider the second type of bad migration, that of hungry ghosts. Hungry ghosts are bereft of food, drink, and resources. In a year they do not use the food, drink, and resources that a human, a god, or an animal uses in a day. A human, god, or animal cannot go a month without eating, never mind a year; we soon die if we do not have food, but due to the force of our own actions, as hungry ghosts we do not die even though we do not have food for years. We continually experience the great suffering of looking for but not finding food and drink. If we think to drink water, we go to the shore of a lake and the lake dries, turning into a beach, or the water turns into undrinkable filth.

It is said in Buddhist scriptures that even if a human puts a cup of water on the table, a hungry ghost sees it as blood, pus, and filth;

a god sees it as ambrosia and a human sees it as water. These three ways of viewing the same liquid are due to three types of actions.

Among the two types of hungry ghosts, the gullet of one is blocked, tied in a knot, and the neck is very long. Usually they cannot find resources to use, and even if they do find food, it will not go down their throats. This is the suffering of hungry ghosts.

I have offered you in brief the story of why gods and humans are said to be the best from among the realm of the transient world. There are six types of migrators in cyclic existence. Hell beings, hungry ghosts and animals are called bad migrations, and humans, demi-gods and gods are called happy migrations. Sometimes we say there are only five types of migrations, including demi-gods in the gods and animals.

The best body and resources are enjoyed by gods and humans. The ranks of humans and gods are called high status. High status in general is of two types. The ultimate high status is to attain the rank of a Buddha and have the body, resources, environment, and companions of a Buddha. High status within cyclic existence are the body, resources, environment, and companions of gods and humans.

In order to attain the high status of a god or a human, you must practice the ten virtues. This is why Buddha said, "Look at your present body to determine what you did in the past. Look at your present mind to determine what will come in the future." Through practicing virtues in the past, the rank, resources, environment, and companions of a god or a human are attained; thus what you did in the past is to be seen in the body, resources, environment, and companions of the present. We can know this as the fruit of having accumulated virtues.

Similarly, we can determine what we are to experience in the future by examining our mind now, and in the same way we can determine that there are differences among humans also—quality of country, of food and drink, of resources and so forth. Even though within cyclic existence the ranks of gods and humans are good, we are born here through virtuous causes and through the force of the twelve branches of dependent-arising—taking birth, becoming old, sick and dying. Thus if in the end we do not act virtuously, we will not be reborn as gods or humans, but will be reborn in any of the three bad migrations. Buddha said, "Examine the present mind to determine what will come in the future."

We should examine our minds, for even though it might be good here and now, we must be careful, otherwise we will be born in a bad migration. This repeated birth, aging, sickness, and death is called cyclic existence. Though there might be a little happiness, gradually it turns into suffering. Thus we must develop the wish definitely to leave cyclic existence completely. We must proceed to a state of happiness in which all suffering is extinguished. The wish to do this is called the intention to leave. It is easy to understand this through condensing what is to be discarded as the first two of the four noble truths and condensing what is to be adopted as the last two of the four noble truths.

How is this? This first of the four noble truths is true sufferings. These are the contaminated mental and physical aggregates of hell beings, hungry ghosts, animals, humans, demi-gods, and gods. The contaminated aggregates are generated through the force of contaminated actions and afflictions. Once we are born, we disintegrate moment by moment through their influence; we cannot stay permanently. We are impermanent. Because we cannot stay for a second moment, but disintegrate moment by moment, these true sufferings are miserable.

Impermanent and miserable, true sufferings are empty of being a permanent self or under the control of a permanent self. Also, these are selfless in the sense of their not being a substantially existent or self-sufficient person or under the control of such a person. True sufferings have these four qualities—impermanence, misery, emptiness, and selflessness.

We must search to determine the cause of this repeated birth, aging, sickness, and death. What is the cause? It is the second noble truth, the true sources of suffering.

The sources of suffering are the afflictions—desire, hatred, and ignorance—and actions contaminated with these afflictions. Motivated by the poisons of desire, hatred, and ignorance, we accumulate actions; thus all true sufferings are derived from the afflictions.

Without abandoning the basic causes, there is no way to avoid undergoing suffering. Therefore, the afflictions are called the faults of all sentient beings throughout all space; all sufferings arises in dependence on them. The causes of suffering, the true sources, must be forsaken.

We must generate the wisdom realizing emptiness—the means of abandoning the afflictions. Once the wisdom of emptiness has been attained and then thoroughly cultivated in meditation, we are liberated. Therefore if we wish definitely to leave cyclic existence, desire, hatred, and ignorance must be eliminated from the root; we must attain true cessations such that they will never return again.

In order to attain true cessations of the afflictions, we must cultivate the true paths, the last of the four noble truths: the path of seeing and the path of meditation. Thus if we summarize the very essence of the wish definitely to leave cyclic existence, true suffering and true sources of suffering are to be forsaken, and true cessations and true paths are to be adopted.

If you just think, "May I myself leave cyclic existence," this indeed helps your own aims a little, but it does not pass beyond the path of a being of middling capacity; therefore, you should generate the wish that all sentient beings, yourself and all others, leave cyclic existence. This is a path of a being of greatest capacity, a complete pure path. In order to generate such a complete pure thought, you must know that true sufferings and true sources of suffering both must be abandoned and that true cessations and true paths are to be assumed. Then when you actually practice true paths and attain true cessations, you will definitely be liberated.

The wish to leave cyclic existence means that wherever you are born through the force of contaminated actions and afflictions—whether in the three bad migrations or in the three happy migrations—you, by the power of contaminated actions and afflictions, are born, age, become sick, and die, and you are seeking gradually to become free of this.

Even if detailed understanding has not been formed, merely hearing once about the path establishes predispositions for the path of freedom. What is the value of establishing predispositions? According to the Cittamātra system, predispositions are established on the mind basis of all (ālayavijñāna); then, later, when you meet with appropriate circumstances, these latencies provide the substance for generating the stages of the path.

According to the Svātantrika-Mādhyamika system, there is a subtle mental consciousness that is the person who has travelled from lifetime to lifetime from beginningless cyclic existence until now. The predispositions which are the seeds for freeing oneself from bondage are established on that subtle mental consciousness. Your hearing about the thought of reversal from the world definitely establishes those seeds.

Similarly, in the Prāsaṅgika-Mādhyamika system, potencies are established on the "mere I", which is only imputed by thought and which is reborn from lifetime to lifetime. Then, in the future—in this lifetime or another lifetime—when you hear or think about this doctrine, these potencies will be activated, quickly generating the paths for liberation.

Let me give a brief example. A man came before Buddha wanting to be a monk. Buddha asked the Hearers if the man could become a monk, and they said that he did not have any merit for becoming a monk. The man was distressed and left to throw himself in a river. The Teacher called the man to him and said, "You Hearers have said he has no merit to become a monk, but in a former lifetime he took birth as an ant on top of an elephant's faeces in a pool surrounding a reliquary of a former Buddha. He has the merit of having circumambulated that reliquary." This is definitely stated in Buddha's word, and it is a fact that predispositions can be established merely through hearing doctrine.

Thus today our meditation is concerned with the thought of emergence from pain. You are to think, "I wish to leave cyclic existence. This, continual birth, aging, sickness, and death is not good. I will free myself from misery; I will attain the peace of extinguishment, and having fulfilled my own aims, will cause all sentient beings throughout space to abandon suffering. When I become liberated, I will draw everyone else up to Buddhahood."

Sit in the meditative posture as was explained before, and if your mind is already settled, you may meditate immediately. If not, count your breath until twenty-one. Realize that you must overcome the causes which force you to wander in the six migrations, the afflictions of desire, hatred, and ignorance.

Much more can be said about the intention to leave cyclic existence. I have offered you a little today in connection with the motivation of the aspiration to highest enlightenment for the sake of all sentient beings. You should generate the thought until, like a prisoner being tortured in a prison and about to die seeking release from his terrible situation, you decide that you definitely will free yourself, attaining the peace of extinguishment, forsaking the afflictions which cause you to be born, age, become sick, and die again and again in the six migrations.

As before, take refuge prior to meditation and dedicate the merit after meditation. Refuge is the door of entry to the Buddhist doctrine. Generation of an altruistic aspiration to highest enlightenment is the door of entry to the Mahāyāna. When you take refuge you are asking for help.

6

The Mind of Enlightenment

ᏟᎯᎯᏉ

The best of all meditations are on the three paths to highest enlightenment, called principal paths because there are none superior for freeing oneself and all sentient beings from suffering and joining oneself and all sentient beings to true happiness.

The three paths are the thought definitely to leave cyclic existence, the altruistic aspiration to highest enlightenment for the sake of all sentient beings, and the correct view of emptiness.

The intention to leave cyclic existence is necessary in order to obtain the happiness of the extinction of suffering. Last time, I told you that the causes of suffering are contaminated actions and afflictions and that because desire, hatred, and ignorance create contaminated actions, we must abandon the affliction. Still, despite cultivating the thought of emergence from suffering, if it is not conjoined with an altruistic mind of enlightenment, we will only attain a freedom from suffering; we will not attain the most marvelous and best of attainments, Buddhahood.

However, if the thought of emergence is cultivated in conjunction with an aspiration to highest enlightenment for the sake of all beings, you can attain the rank of a Buddha. There is no doubt.

Even though you meditate on emptiness, if you do not have this altruistic aspiration, you can be freed from suffering, but you will not attain the rank of a Buddha. Therefore, this altruistic aspiration, called the mind of enlightenment, is most important.

If you are able to cultivate all three aspects of the path—the thought definitely to leave cyclic existence, the mind of enlightenment, and the correct view of emptiness—there is no better meditation. In general there are many systems of meditation, and indeed every one of them achieves an effect. The Sāṃkhyas and the other non-Buddhist meditators, in dependence on their meditation attain the rank of gods, attain happiness in this life and rebirth in the formless realm, living happily for many thousands of aeons. It is definite that except for the Nihilists, all systems have such meditations. What is the difference in Buddhism? Even though non-Buddhists attain aeons of happiness, due to not having cultivated the thought to leave cyclic existence, once that happiness is finished, they again fall. The benefit of their meditation is inconceivable, but they still cannot attain liberation.

In just the same way, even within the Buddhist system, those of the Hearer Vehicle and the Solitary Realizer Vehicle cultivate the paths of a being of small or middling capacity and thereby attain liberation, but due to not cultivating the altruistic mind of enlightenment, they cannot attain the rank of a Buddha. Through cultivating the thought to leave cyclic existence, together with the view of emptiness, they are freed from misery, but if they also cultivate the altruistic aspiration, they will also attain the rank of a Buddha. There is no one who cannot attain Buddhahood, if these three paths are cultivated.

If you meditate forcefully on these three, you can attain the rank of a Buddha quickly, but even if you cannot meditate forcefully, a small amount of meditation will establish predispositions in this lifetime. Then when you meditate in the next lifetime, you will proceed very quickly, just like the Tibetan yogi, Milarepa.

Today I will offer you a little on the altruistic mind of enlightenment which is to be cultivated in conjunction with the intention to leave the world suffering.

In Buddhism there are two ways of cultivating the mind of enlightenment. One was passed from Buddha to Maitreya who transmitted it to Asaṅga; this is the sevenfold cause and effect precepts—recognizing all sentient beings as mothers, being mindful of their kindness, intending to repay their kindness, love, compassion, unusual attitude, and altruistic mind of enlightenment itself.

The other way of generating the same mind of enlightenment is through the precepts passed from Buddha to Mañjuśrī who transmitted them to Nāgārjuna. It is called equalizing and switching self and other. First, you cease liking yourself so much and mistreating others by considering both self and others equal. Then you switch the endearment that you have for yourself to others and switch the non-endearment and desertion that you have for others to yourself.

Although there are these two modes of meditation, that which is being cultivated is just an altruistic mind of enlightenment. The mind of enlightenment in general is divided into two types, conventional and ultimate. The conventional mind of enlightenment is divided again into the aspirational and the practical.

The aspirational mind of enlightenment means to reflect on the switching of self and other or the seven-fold cause and effect precepts and thereby develop the wish to attain the rank of a Buddha in order to help all sentient being.

The practical mind of enlightenment comes when, having generated the altruistic aspiration to Buddhahood, you engage in the four means of gathering students and the six perfections and thereby begin accumulating the collections of merit and wisdom.

The actual aspirational mind of enlightenment is begun with the path of accumulation and continues until the stage of Buddhahood. The practical goes along with it. The aspirational has twenty-one different forms called "like earth," "like gold," and so forth, which are instances of its increasing higher and higher, stronger and stronger, as one progresses. However, they are all just this one conventional mind of enlightenment.

An ultimate mind of enlightenment is a wisdom consciousness in meditative equipoise directly cognizing emptiness at the time of attaining a Mahāyāna path of seeing.

Today from among the different types of the mind of enlightenment, I will talk about the conventional, and among its different types, I will explain how to cultivate in meditation the aspiration mind of enlightenment.

There are seven steps: recognition of all sentiment beings as mothers, being mindful of their kindness, intending to repay their kindness, love, compassion, unusual attitude, and altruistic mind of enlightenment itself. These steps are to be preceded by cultivating evenmindedness. The reason for this is that other persons are definitely in three categories: one group whom we like, one group to whom we display anger, as if they were enemies, and one group who has neither helped nor harmed us in this lifetime, such as birds, bugs, and some humans.

The reason why you should first cultivate equanimity is that if you jump to the first step, trying to recognize all sentient beings as mothers and become mindful of their kindness, it will be impossible to recognize an enemy as having been your mother in the past. Also, if you try to apply it to your friends, you will not think of them as having been mothers; you will generate desire and your meditation will not succeed. Therefore, think first about a neutral person, someone who is not an enemy, not your father or mother, member of your family, or friend and think, "Now this person neither likes me nor dislikes me, but in a former lifetime, this person was my mother and just as my mother of this lifetime helped me, so he was very kind. Even though he does not presently like or dislike me, I must remember his former kindness now."

Even though in the past he also became angry and was your enemy, it is his kindness when he was your mother that you are to remember. Not discarding him, you should consider him equal to your parents of this lifetime. Then imagining him in front of you, you should think, "He wants happiness and does not want unhappiness, but over the course of lifetimes, through holding me as intimate, he has helped and sometimes, through holding me as distant, has harmed. Thus how nice it would be if both he and I could become free of desire and hatred, intimacy and alienness and abide in an even-mindedness toward each other. May the lamas and gods empower me to do this."

I will tell you why you should request empowerment from the lamas and gods to do this. When Buddha was in his eighty-first year, had taught the eighty-four thousand masses of practice, and was about to die, Mañjuśrī and Vajrapāṇi asked him, "Now you are about to pass away. After you have passed away and when we seek explanations on meditation, in whom should we place our confidence? Whose speech should we accept?"

Buddha said, "In the future, I will abide in the form of teachers. At that time, believe in the teacher with faith that he is I, generate the firm faith thinking that he is the teacher, Śākyamuni. It will be the same as receiving doctrine from Buddha himself. Thus, we make prayer petitions such as, "May we come to have an evenmindedness free of desire and hatred and intimacy and alienness, and to do this we ask the lamas and gods for their blessed empowerment."

The second step is to imagine a pleasant sentient being in front of you and to think, "Although he is pleasant now, he was my enemy in the past, and thus I should consider him equal with the neutral being. Except that now I like him due to the force of desire, he and the neutral person, whom I presently neither desire nor hate, have no difference at all."

Then imagine an enemy in front of you and think, "That I do not like him now is due to his having harmed me, and except for that, he—like the others—was my parent in the past and took care of me with kindness. My relatives and friends, except for acting nicely toward me now, harmed me in the past. Thus they are all the same."

If you meditate this way for a long time, then even when you see an enemy, he will be no different from a friend. You will think, "Even though he is harming me now, he was my friend in the past." Even when you see a friend, you will think, "Except that we desire each other now, in the past this person was my enemy," And even when you see your own parents, you will think, "They are nice to me in this lifetime, but in the past they were my enemies and thus are no different from the others." This is called evenmindedness, not allowing a particular relationship of the moment to serve as a cause for desire or hatred with regard to any sentient being anywhere.

This acts as the cause of the effect of being able to recognize all sentient being as the closest of all your relatives, your mother. You realize that your enemy of the present was once your best of friends, that your best of friends was once your enemy, and that neutral people were both the closest of friends and the greatest of enemies. "Thus they are all the same without the slightest difference, and when each and every one of them was my mother, they had great kindness for me."

You should keep meditating until you experience all sentient beings, from bugs on up, as having been your mother in the past. There is not any sentient being who was not your mother in the past.

If you had attempted this thought immediately without preparing its ground through attaining even-mindedness, you would not have succeeded. When you saw an enemy, you would get angry. When you saw a close friend, you would generate desire; when you saw a neutral human, a bug or an animal, you would just not think anything. For instance, when a friend dies or is sick, we are extremely sad; when an enemy dies or becomes sick, we are glad and even wish him more suffering, and when a neutral person gets sick or dies, we just think, "Oh," and do not pay any attention to it. Unlike that, you should make everyone equal.

All other living beings are only your own parents, either in this lifetime itself or in former lifetimes. When you become mindful of this equally toward all sentient beings, this is called the recognition of the mothers. It is the first of the seven cause and effect precepts for generating a mind of enlightenment. When you arrive at the point of recognizing all sentient beings as your own mother, then this first cause has been generated in your mental continuum. It produces an effect which is the second step, being mindful of their kindness. We will talk about it later.

When you meditate, ask for help from the Three Jewels to realize that all other living beings are either your parents of this lifetime or were your parents in other lifetimes. Since this is the door of generating the mind of enlightenment, its benefit has no boundary or measure although it is not physical; if it were, it would not fit into this whole country. Later, when you have trained more, you will know the great benefit of this meditation.

Thank you. If you have any questions, please ask them.

Q.   When we visualize a sentient being, is it better to visualize a human or an animal?

A.   It is good to visualize a human, but it is also good to visualize an animal, such as a cow. In books it only says to visualize a sentient being; it does not specify a human, a cow, a hell being, or a hungry ghost.

Q.   If one's parents have been unkind, can we substitute another friend who has been helpful?

A.   Your parents have been extremely kind. Your parents copulated, and you took birth inside your mother's womb. You stayed there for nine months and several days, and your body was formed. You emerged from the mother's womb and because you were much like a bug at that time, if your mother had not taken care of you, you would not now know how to talk. In Tibet there was a case of children who were left without care. The father and brothers had to work and later, when the children became adults, they would go begging, but they could only grunt. From the time of conception in the womb to leaving school, parents extend great help. Based on this you later can become a teacher or even a president. This is the kindness of their having taken care of you until age twenty. If our parents had not taken care of us, our lives would be wasted.

7

The Mothers' Kindness

ﾟ◌ﾟ

From among the three principal paths to highest enlightenment, we have been talking about the altruistic mind of enlightenment. Last time, from among the seven cause and effect precepts, I offered the recognition of all sentient beings as mothers; today, the second step is to become mindful of their kindness.

Of what kindness are you to become mindful? Just as your parents of this lifetime extended kindness to you, so all sentient beings—even though they might not be helping you in this lifetime—were just as as helpful in former lifetimes. You should cultivate this thougaht in meditation—first with respect to your own very kind parents of this lifetime, then with respect to neutral beings who have neither harmed nor helped you, and then to your enemies.

The essence of this meditation is to become aware that even if persons presently are enemies or neutral or even friends, they are as kind to you as your own parents of this lifetime. That is the essence of the meditation.

What is the kindness of your mother? First of all, we enter into the mother's womb while our parents are copulating. During the first week we stay in the mother's womb not knowing anything, with our mind entered into this jelly-like substance of the father's semen and the mother's blood.

During the second week the fetus becomes a little hard. Unlike water or blood, it is now like yogurt. During the third week, the fetus becomes roundish, and during the succeeding weeks bumps appear which develop into the various limbs—head, arms and legs. Then we grow stage by stage over many weeks. During that time, inside our mother's womb, we are not aware of her physical and mental discomfort.

After nine months and several days, we are born. During birth the mother is extremely uncomfortable, and we ourselves prior to birth and during birth have indescribable discomfort due to the way the mother lies down, eats, and so forth. Still, the mother considers the child in her own womb more important than even her own body. Thinking, "My child will be harmed," she makes great effort at eating, sleeping, and moving about properly. Aside from suffering, she is not comfortable at all.

When we are about to be reborn, we turn around inside the womb and begin to come out, causing the mother such pain that she almost faints. Our very emergence from the womb causes her vagina to be torn. Then the unbilical cord between the womb of the mother and the navel of the child must be cut.

The mother's vagina has been ripped, her body has been harmed, and she has undergone such suffering, but she does not throw us away as we would throw away feces, but cherishes and takes care of us. Her kindness for the sake of her child is greater than the endearment she has for her own life. Her kindness is very great.

Consider the marvelous ways your mother held you, was pleasant to you, held you to her flesh, gave you milk. Though she valued you more than her own life, the only way that you can know what she did for you during the first year or two, is to watch a mother take care of her child. Unless you have great concentration you cannot remember the many forms of her kindness. Since we had not studied then, if our mothers had told us to do this or that, we could not have understood. Except that we had the shape of a human, we were like bugs. She taught us each word, one by one, how to eat, how to sleep, how to put on clothes, how to urinate, and how to defecate. If she had not taught us these and had let us alone, we would still be like bugs. In time you will know this clearly. When the young girls among you give birth you will think, "Oh, what he said before is just true." It is not only clear that among humans parents are very kind to their sons and daughters, but also even if a cat gives birth to a kitten, we can see with our own eyes that the cat will undergo great difficulties to take care of the kitten until it is able to go on its own.

There are many ways in which a mother extends kindness to her child, and I have mentioned a few briefly. Just as our mothers extended great kindness to us in this lifetime, so those who presently seem to be enemies—not liking us—were our mother in a former life and have been very kind to us. Therefore you should not become angry thinking, "Such and such a person is my enemy." Even if he acted as an enemy in this lifetime, in a former lifetime he acted as your mother. And, in a later lifetime, like your mother of this lifetime, he will protect you with kindness. If it were necessary to become angry when you think someone is your enemy, then since your mother of this lifetime was your enemy in a former lifetime and will be your enemy in a future lifetime, then you should hate her. That is how you should think.

Then consider a neutral being who in this lifetime neither liked you as in the case of your parents, nor disliked you as in the case of an enemy—someone like a cow.

You should not think that this person has not helped you, for in a former lifetime he protected you with kindness just like your mother of this lifetime. Therefore, you should think, "Even though so and so is neutral now, he was my mother in the past and will be my mother in the future. He helped me in the past and will help me in the future."

Again, you should not generate great desire for someone and think that he is just good. The person was an enemy in the past and will be an enemy in the future. You should consider them all equally.

If you do not consider them all equally—if you do not consider their kindness in the past—you will be fondling and kissing your enemy, eating your father's flesh, and throwing a stone at your mother's head as in the story I told you before.

Our enemies of today all were our parents in the past. You should not be too attached to persons, even your own husband or wife, relatives or friends, liking them too much. Perhaps they were enemies in the past.

You should consider equally the kindness of everyone over your long span of lifetimes. You should not become angry when a little thing goes wrong. You should think of the kind help the person has given you. For instance, if your parents or another friend of this lifetime, who has helped you a great deal, does something unsuitable or even slaps you, it is wrong to respond with harsh words, throwing him away. If you anger, thinking, "He slapped me!" it is not at all suitable. If you do not repay the great kindness that others have offered you, it is much like taking out a loan, obtaining food, drink and resources through it, and then not repaying it. Through the force of such an action you will suffer in the future. Therefore discard hating those who harm you. Cast aside the thought, "This one has not helped me in this lifetime." Think instead, "Each and every one of these beings, upon taking birth in cyclic existence over the-beginningless continuum of lives, has protected me with kindness just as my own parents in this lifetime. Again in the future, when they take rebirth in cyclic existence, they will help me when they are my parents."

The first of the seven steps is to experience all other sentient beings as having been your mother, and the second is this knowledge of their great kindness. The third is the intent to repay their kindness. "I will engage in the means to cause all to have happiness and to be free of suffering. Just as they helped me in the past, now I must help them."

What do they need? What is the way to repay their kindness? You should cause them to become free of suffering and to possess happiness because the worst of all situations is that they have taken birth in cyclic existence. "I will engage in the means to liberate them from suffering. It would be extremely shameful, lawless, and nauseous if, once they had helped me so much, I forgot their kindness and did not make effort to the means of freeing them."

You should make a petition to the Three Jewels asking for help in cultivating this intention.

What is liberation? Living beings are born as gods and humans, or if they have accumulated non-virtues, as animals, hungry ghosts, and hell beings. Until we become free of cyclic existence, we ourselves and all others must undergo repeated birth, aging, sickness, and death over and over. Therefore, we must identify the material causes of cyclic existence. These are contaminated actions and afflictions. Motivated by the afflictions we accumulate actions; therefore desire, hatred and ignorance are the causes of bondage. The afflictions in anyone's continuum, your own or another's, are the enemies of all sentient beings throughout space.

Attachment is generated to objects of desire, and then when we think that we have been wronged, we hate and kill and fight each other. Through the force of anger there is always war in the world. Even if we do not kill, we wreck each other, and the fault is due to initially arousing hatred against the other person. Ignorance means to be obscured and to enter into actions in a confused state, not knowing that if such is done fault will occur or that if such and such is done fault will not occur. It makes us err.

Therefore, desire, hatred, and ignorance cause all sentient beings throughout space to migrate in cyclic existence, to become angry, and to become attached; thus, the afflictions are called the enemies of all sentient beings throughout space. A person who has abandoned them is called a Foe Destroyer. Overcoming his foe, he is liberated from cyclic existence. Being without the afflictions, even if he has countless predispositions formed over his beginningless span of lifetimes for becoming a hell being, hungry ghost, animal, human, demi-god, or god, he cannot take rebirth in cyclic existence. Even if you have the seeds of rice or wheat, if you do not have water, earth, and warmth, then rice and wheat will not grow. In the same way, if you are able to abandon the afflictions, you cannot be born by the power of karma—the actions you have accumulated formerly. You will be freed from birth, aging, sickness, and death. This is called the bliss of the extinguishment of suffering.

The intent to do this is called the thought definitely to leave cyclic existence. In summary, all living beings—as illustrated by our parents of this lifetime—have protected us with kindness; in return for their kindness we are engaging in meditation for the sake of establishing them in liberation, the bliss of extinguishment of all misery.

Now that we have recognized all sentient beings as mothers and are mindful of their kindness, our meditation today is to cultivate the prayer petition, "May all sentient beings be set in the bliss of liberation." If you cultivate this properly with respect to all beings throughout space, the benefits are very great. But even if you merely generate the suspicion that doing such would help, it makes weaker the sins and obstructions which cause rebirth in cyclic existence. If you meditate only once, "May all sentient beings be liberated from the suffering of cyclic existence and attain the bliss of liberation," this is more powerful than cultivating for hundreds of thousands of years a wish for merely your own liberation.

The physical posture for meditation is as I mentioned before and there are two types of engagement of the mind, analytical meditation and stabilizing meditation. Analytical meditation means to investigate and analyze an object—for instance, analyzing the reasons for repaying the kindness of sentient beings—whereas stabilizing meditation is just to set the mind on one object without such analysis. However, you need to analyze during both types of meditation in the sense of watching your mind carefully. Otherwise, you will become dizzy and sleep. If the motivation of your meditation is altruistic, then it will help both yourself and others. If you have any questions, please ask them.

Q. Why should we not become angry at others when they harm us?

A. If your mother, who has been so extremely kind to you for so many years, became incensed and tried to attack you, would you become angry at her and start beating her, or would you try to calm her down and seek a means to restore her mind to her usual state? In the same way, another sentient being who is angry at you is only your own best friend who has lost control of himself and, without independence, is attacking you. He is not at fault, he is not acting under his own power. He has helped you before and will help you again. When you were inside his.womb, how much suffering he underwent? Then after you were born, how many difficulties he had to bear! We do not remember the difficulties our mothers had to undergo during our first few years. Except for those who have clairvoyance, we do not have a measure of the suffering that our mother has undergone for our sake. Therefore first it is important to gain a measure of her kindness in this lifetime and then see all others in this way.

8

Altruism

ᘓᘏᘓ

From among the seven-fold cause and effect precepts, I have explained recognition of all sentient beings as mothers, mindfulness of their kindness and intention to repay their kindness. Today I will offer fourth precept, love.

In relation to what field of awareness are we cultivating love? The field of awareness is all sentient beings. What are the aspects of a consciousness cultivating love? There are three. One is the thought, "How nice it would be if all sentient beings had happiness." The second is, "May all sentient beings have happiness," and the third is, "I will cause all sentient beings to have happiness."

As Buddha says in the King of Meditations Sūtra, the benefit of cultivating love with all sentient beings as your field of awareness is extremely great. It is a thousand times greater or even immeasurably greater than the benefit of making offerings over many aeons, offering whole lands filled with food, drink, and articles. Even if such offering is made in the best of lands, it would be far more beneficial to cultivate love here in our world. Also, in the Sūtra of Mañjuśrī's Land, Buddha says that there is a Buddha land to the northeast of this world which is unlike anything else. Beings there are extremely happy because they have attained cessation of coarse feelings and discriminations, abiding most comfortably in meditative stabilization without any suffering. Being so happy, they find it very easy to engage in pure behavior for many thousands of ten millions of years. They do not kill, steal, engage in sexual misconduct, and so forth. Buddha said that although the benefit of their practice is great, it is more beneficial to cultivate love here for the time it takes to snap the fingers.

Thus if there is such benefit in taking cognizance of all sentient beings and cultivating the thought, even for a snapping of the fingers, "May they have happiness," then we could not explain how much benefit there would be if we cultivated love for an hour or a week. The reason for the greatness of the benefit is that the field of thought is vast, and we are realizing our intimate relationship with all these beings through recognizing them as mothers, becoming mindful of their kindness, and intending to repay their kindness.

How is love cultivated in meditation? The three aspects of a loving consciousness, which are three levels of increasing strength, are to be cultivated in thought again and again:

"How nice it would be if all sentient beings had happiness and the causes of happiness."

"May all sentient beings have happiness and the causes of happiness."

"I will cause all sentient beings to have happiness and the causes of happiness."

First, take as your object of awareness a friend or your father or mother and cultivate the wish that this person have happiness. When you gain facility with that, then take as your object a sentient being who is neither a friend nor an enemy and, as before, cultivate the wish that this person have happiness and the causes of happiness. When you develop facility, take as your object of awareness someone who seems to be an enemy in this lifetime, who does not like you, who is disagreeable to you, and cultivate love until there is no difference between the wish for happiness that you have for the first two and for your enemy. This person in the past was as kind to you as your own parents of this lifetime. He has arisen as your enemy now due to the force of the afflictions—desire, hatred, and ignorance. Thus, there is no cause for anger, and even more, you should develop a strong thought, "May he have happiness."

When you develop facility such that the wish comes equally toward all three types of beings, then extend your meditation slowly to all sentient beings throughout space. During your gradual progress in cultivating the three wishes, you need to reflect again and again on the disadvantages of their not having happiness and the advantages of their having happiness. The true thought, "May they have happiness," is far more beneficial to sentient beings than making gifts to them of gold, silver and jewels filling several world systems. Also, even if you gave gold, silver and jewels to them, filling several rooms, you could not keep yourself from thinking, "Oh I have given such and such great things to these people."

Here, rather than thinking that you have given something great to other people, you are first reflecting on the great kindness that they have given you, and in return you are cultivating the thought, "May they have happiness and the causes of happiness." Just as sentient beings are limitless, so the benefit of such meditation is limitless. One benefit is that due to having helped others, even only in thought, in future lifetimes everyone will be good to you, and the conditions of your lives will be most marvelous. There will be no one to harm you. Like planting a field, your own cultivation of love yields a harvest of beneficial relationships.

Thus I have given you a brief account of how to cultivate love. We have finished the first four of the seven precepts, recognition of all sentient beings as mothers, becoming mindful of their kindness, intending to repay their kindness, and love. This means that, having cultivated love, you will find a sense of pleasantness in each and every sentient being irregardless of their external qualities.

Please cultivate love step by step.

9
Great Compassion

CRO

Today I will offer you the steps for cultivating compassion. What is the field of awareness of compassionate mind? The field of awareness is all sentient beings who have any of the three types of suffering—the suffering of pain, the suffering of change, and the suffering of being so composed as to bae always ready to undergo pain. Among these are included birth, aging, sickness, and death. Wherever you are born—in a bad migration or in a happy migration—once you take birth by the power of contaminated actions and afflictions, in the end there is nothing to come except suffering. Many billions of years have passed since this world was formed. Since then all of us have been born, aged, become sick, and died again and again without interruption. There is no one among us who has managed just to stay alive. We died and took rebirth over and over.

Sufferings of change are feelings of pleasure which, when we superficially consider them, seem to be pleasure, but they can change into suffering. Let me illustrate it with an easy example. If people like us go out in the sun where it is too hot, we are pleased when we go to a cooler spot, but if we stay there long, we will become cold and sick. Similarly, when we become too cold and go to a hot place, again, if we become too hot, we become sick. Although there is a seeming pleasure of becoming cooler or warmer, if we remain in it too long, it turns into suffering. This shows that these experiences do not have an inherent nature of pleasure.

Similarly, if we like an enjoyable food too much and eat too much, even though it is delicious, we will become sick. If we eat a huge quantity, eventually our stomach will ache, we will throw up, and have a country full of problems.

Similarly, in this world—whether it be animals or humans—

beings mate and copulate with pleasure, but if it is not done in a moderate amount, the male's semen will be finished and blood will come out. This causes a disease called cold and wind in the lower abdomen, and it harms both male and female genitals making a great deal of trouble. Though it is enjoyable at first, it can ruin the very basis of comfort in our vessels. This is put forth in Dharmakīrti's Commentary on (Dignāga's) "Compendium on Valid Cognition." These seem to be pleasurable, but over a long period of time they turn into suffering itself. Thus these feelings of contaminated pleasure are called sufferings of change.

The third type of suffering is called the suffering of pervasive composition. Wherever a sentient being takes birth by the power of contaminated actions and afflictions in the desire realm, form realm, or formless realm, there are periods when he does not have manifest suffering. However, if certain conditions aggregate, suffering will be generated. This suffering is called suffering of pervasive composition, because the causes of suffering pervade all types of life within the three realms, and thus the beings in the three realms are ready to suffer when minor conditions or causes aggregate.

Our composition is such that with causes of suffering pervading our structure, we are prepared to undergo suffering even if it is not manifest now. For instance, we have no suffering now, but if we are stuck with a needle or cut with a knife or kicked, pain is immediately generated.

Thus all sentient beings have these three types of suffering. Taking cognizance of them as your field of awareness, you should cultivate compassion, thinking, "May all sentient beings be free of suffering and the causes of suffering."

The aspects of a compassionate consciousness are three. The first and weaker form is the thought, "How nice it would be if all sentient beings were free of suffering and the causes of suffering." Then the stronger aspect is, "May all sentient beings be free of suffering and the causes of suffering." The strongest aspect is, "I will cause all sentient beings to be free of suffering and the causes of suffering."

In the process of generating compassion it is necessary to recognize suffering, and in your recognition of suffering you should first think not about others, but about yourself. You should think, "I have engaged in the non-virtues since beginningless time and have accumulated bad karma. I suffer pain. I suffer change. I am afflicted by being always liable to suffer pain." Think of the causes of suffering, the ten non-virtues, and how you have engaged in them, and think about how you have suffering in this lifetime.

Such thought does not generate compassion. It generates an intention to leave cyclic existence. when you realize that you are in such a state, you will see that there is nothing else to do except attain liberation, extricating yourself from the process of birth which is under the influence of contaminated actions and afflictions. You will know that just as you have suffered in this lifetime, once you die the process will begin again and that wherever you are born—even as a god or a human—you must undergo the sufferings of birth, aging, sickness, and death. You will generate an intention to leave cyclic existence completely and forever.

Once you have felt this with respect to yourself, you should consider your father and mother of this lifetime. They have the three types of suffering and they have the causes of suffering. Even when they finish undergoing the suffering of this lifetime, they will have more in the next lifetime. When you think this, compassion will be generated.

Thus, first of all, consider yourself. The benefits of doing so are indeed small compared to considering others; however, in order to generate an understanding of others' suffering, it is necessary first to know the great immeasurable fault of your own birth in cyclic existence.

Once you have a clear sense of your own situation, take as your object of awareness your own mother, a relative, or very close friend, and cultivate compassion wishing that this person be free of suffering and the causes of suffering. When you attain facility, cultivate it with respect to a neutral person; then take cognizance of an enemy, and later extend the meditation slowly to all sentient beings.

You should cultivate compassion gradually in these stages, first considering a friend, then a neutral person, and then an enemy. Otherwise, if you merely think, "May all sentient beings have happiness and the causes of happiness," then when a misfortune such as death occurs to your enemy, you will automatically think, "Oh, misfortune has befallen him. That's just right." Similarly, if misfortune such as death strikes a neutral person—someone who is neither friend nor enemy—you will just think, "Oh, did he die?" and cast aside any further thought on the subject. Again, if you do not consider friends, neutral people, and enemies to be equal, then even if a friend merely becomes a little sick, you will almost go crazy. Therefore, create in meditation an even-mindedness, an equality toward friends and neutral people.

When an even-mindedness has been achieved, then extend your meditation to enemies. When friends, neutral beings, and enemies have been equalized, you will value them equally, equally good and equally bad, unable to say that such and such is worse.

If you do not create a sense of equality among people and become accustomed to it, there is no way for meditation to succeed. There will be no way for you to wish happiness equally for friends, neutral persons, and enemies. But if you can equalize them, then everyone will be no different from your own mother.

Why should you make all neutral persons and enemies equal to your mother? For instance, if she had fallen into a ravine, or into a river or had fallen into a crack in the earth made by an earthquake, and if her own sons and daughters would not help her up, who would help her?

Why is this? If the child, whom she had helped from the time of its entry into her womb until nowadays, would not help her when she fell unconscious in a ditch by the road, who would help her? If you did not help your mother up onto the road, take her to the hospital and so forth, if you did not act so as to bring happiness in all of your future lifetimes, repaying her kindness, you would be shameless. Never mind in terms of religious practice, even in the world a son or daughter, who does not help a parent and instead abandons them when they are undergoing great difficulty, is a bad person and is to be removed from the count of humans. Not only does such a person have no religious thought, but also when his parents are undergoing suffering from being sick or having fallen into a ravine, he does not help, but perhaps stands by and laughs. Everyone would consider him shameless. It is commonly thought that such sons and daughters, when they have children, will have children who do the same to them.

Thus, the fifth step is meditation of compassion in which you cultivate equally toward all sentient beings the thought, "May they be free of suffering and the causes of suffering."

Again, the aspects of a compassionate consciousness are of three types. The small type of compassion in the thought, "How nice it would be if all sentient beings were free of suffering and the causes of suffering." The middling compassion is the wish, "May all sentient beings be free from suffering and the causes of suffering," and the greatest compassion is the intention, "I will cause all sentient beings throughout space, as illustrated by my father and mother of this lifetime, to be free of suffering and the causes of suffering. I ask for blessed empowerment from the lamas and the Three Jewels to enable me to do this."

This meditation has great benefits, and you yourself will know them in the future. Assume the meditative posture and consider a parent or a close friend, a neutral person, and then an enemy—finally extending your compassion to all.

Because the benefits of cultivating compassion in meditation for even the period of a snapping of fingers are so great, if you cultivate it for a few minutes, the benefit is beyond measure. I am not just saying something pretty. Read Buddha's word, search it out, and practice—you will come to believe it.

If you have any questions, please ask them.

Q. Should we again today recognize all sentient beings as mothers, become mindful of their kindness, intend to repay their kindness, and generate love?

A. It is best to abbreviate the first four steps, thinking, "All were my mothers, they were extremely kind to me; their kindness should be repaid. May they have happiness and the causes of happiness."Having thought those briefly, then pass on to compassion, "May they be free from suffering and the causes of suffering."

Q. In meditation today, we are first concentrating on a friend, then a neutral person, and then an enemy. Originally when generating even-mindedness, we first took cognizance of a neutral being. What is the reason for the change in order?

A. Without meditation, you have a similitude of even-mindedness toward a neutral being, free of desire and hatred. Therefore, when attempting to generate equanimity even with respect to friends and enemies, first you should get used to it with an easy object. You actually have only a similitude of even-mindedness or equanimity toward the neutral person because your equanimity is an equanimity of desertion, not desiring and not hating but also not valuing a neutral person. Still, when the goal is to generate even-mindedness, you should begin with a being toward whom it is easy to generate.

We abbreviated the preliminary step of generating even-mindedness and the step of recognizing all sentient beings as mothers into one meditation. Actually, when you reflect on the fact that all sentient beings have been your mother in former lifetimes it is best to begin with a friend, not with a neutral person. However, since we blended the two meditations, seeking even-mindedness by means of recognizing all sentient beings as having been mothers, we began with a neutral being. In the meditations of love and compassion, you begin with a friend because it is extremely easy to wish that a friend be free of suffering and joined with happiness. The consequences of a friend's having suffering and not having happiness are more obvious to us. Therefore, you should begin with a friend, and having developed facility with respect to the friend, you are able to measure your progress easily with respect to a neutral person and an enemy by comparing it to your strong feeling for your friend.

We live in the degenerate era near the time of the end of Buddhist teaching. When I think about the benefit of our gathering and talking together here at such a time, I am very happy. Your fortune is immeasurable.

10

The Unusual Attitude

The sixth of the seven-fold cause and effect precepts for generating a mind of enlightenment is called the unusual attitude.

It indeed is meditation of love and compassion, but because love and compassion are cultivated here with a special force this is called the unusual attitude. What is it?

Formerly, through seeing that all sentient beings do not have happiness but remain tortured by suffering, you developed love and compassion. Here when cultivating the unusual attitude, its special force is that you think, "I alone take upon myself the burden of causing all sentient beings to be free from suffering and the causes of suffering."

The mere thought, "How nice it would be," or "May they have these," is not sufficient. "Being a son or a daughter of all these sentient beings, if I did not make effort at the means to cause them to have happiness, I would be shameless. I would be vulgar in the eyes of the world. The Buddhas of the ten directions would consider me to be without purpose."

Thus we should take upon ourselves the burden of freeing all sentient beings from suffering and joining them with happiness. For instance, if your own parents become impoverished, lacking food and drink, you as their sons and daughters should assume the task of caring for them. Similarly, when this unusual attitude of compassion is cultivated in meditation, you are the child who was helped by each and every sentient being, and those sentient beings— your parents—have as if fallen into a river or a ravine, with their legs broken, and if you left them in such a state you would be shameless. In this meditation you take upon yourself the burden of freeing all beings throughout space from suffering and the causes of suffering. The mind willing to assume this burden is called the unusual attitude of compassion.

This is to be cultivated not only in meditative session but also after loosening yourself from the session when going, staying, eating, working, or sleeping. Even though you might be working, in the depths of the mind the force of your thought, "I will cause all sentient beings to be free from suffering and to be joined with happiness," remains, unable to be destroyed. This is the unusual attitude.

Why is this? Let me illustrate it with an example. If the very bitter bark of a tree is mixed with a few drops of molasses or sugar, the bitterness will not be relieved; it will not be sweet at all. In the same way, mere occasional cultivation of the thoughts of love and compassion will not become the unusual attitude, but if you meditate frequently and over a long time, it will. Thus the mark of having generated the unusual attitude is that in all modes of behavior this assumption of the burden of freeing all from suffering and joining all with happiness remains inseparably and incontrovertibly with your mind.

When anyone attains this unusual attitude, he has entered among the beings of greatest capacity from among the three types of beings—small, middling, and great.

This being has abandoned his own aims and is intent on the welfare of others, working only for the aims of all sentient beings throughout space. Even if the Hearers and Solitary Realizers reach the end of their paths and become Foe Destroyers, they are still not beings of greatest capacity. Foe Destroyers themselves must train their minds in recognition of all sentient beings as mothers, mindfulness of their kindness, intention to repay their kindness, love, compassion, and the unusual attitude. When they generate the unusual attitude, they are called "Those who formerly generated the realization of a Foe Destroyer," but they are no longer actual Foe Destroyers. They have become beings of greatest capacity.

When trainees have arrived at the stage wherein their training in the unusual attitude has been completed and cannot be forgotten, they wonder what special means there are to bring about the welfare of all beings. Even if there is benefit in merely cultivating these thoughts in meditation, one needs to know the means by which sentient beings can be freed from suffering and joined with happiness; otherwise, it is only a wish. Thus they search to see who has such means. They discover that those who have such marvelous means have the rank of a blessed Buddha.

For them to come to this decision, they must develop faith in the qualities of a Buddha. In the sūtras and commentaries there are three types of faith, of which the lowest is called the faith of clear delight. It is like burning a light in the mind. It is like a jewel put in a lake which settles out all the dirt. It is a state of simple delight in a virtuous object. The second is the faith of knowledgeable belief. For instance, it is faith in the cause and effect of actions based on knowledge that from engaging in virtues, happiness will arise and from engaging in non-virtues, suffering will arise.

Let us take an example from what we can see with our own eyes. If we have made great effort in learning how to run a machine in a factory or in learning a subject in school, we will have a knowledgeable belief that there are definite beneficial results in such training.

The cause and effect of actions do exist but cannot be seen with the eyes; however, from our own experience and through reasoning, we can develop knowledgeable belief in the cause and effect of actions. Similarly, in this case, we can develop the knowledgeable belief that our intentions of helping sentient beings can be fulfilled if we attain the rank of a Buddha—as in the case of Śākyamuni Buddha who originally generated an aspiration to highest enlightenment and then for three countless aeons accumulated the collections of merit and wisdom, and finally became fully and perfectly enlightened into the body, speech, mind, qualities, and activities of a Buddha.

In brief, when we have discovered that a Buddha has abandoned all that is to be abandoned and has attained all that is to be attained, we will come to believe that there is great purpose in attaining the rank of a Buddha. Once we believe in Buddhahood, we will generate the third type of faith, the wish to attain such a state.

Thus, based on faith, those who have generated the unusual attitude see that a Buddha has all the means necessary to effect their wish to help all sentient beings. They examine their own lives and see that now, never mind helping others, they cannot even free themselves; they have not even freed themselves from suffering and the causes of suffering. Therefore, they ascertain with valid cognition that they must attain Buddhahood; they see clearly the necessity of attaining Buddhahood. Then, they look into their own minds to see if it is possible to attain Buddhahood. Through careful study of emptiness, they see that the nature of the mind is not naturally defiled with desire, hatred, and ignorance, but that these are peripheral factors and the nature of the mind is intrinsically pure. Thus they ascertain with valid cognition that they can attain Buddhahood.

They have taken upon themselves the burden of the welfare of all sentient beings, and they have seen that they must and can attain Buddhahood. At this point they have arrived at the seventh of the seven-fold cause and effect precepts, the actual altruistic aspiration to highest enlightenment itself. At this point they promise to attain the rank of a Buddha. This is the actualization of an aspirational mind of enlightenment.

Maitreya in his Ornament for the Realizations says, "The mind of enlightenment is the wish for complete perfect enlightenment for the sake of others." It is the thought, "I will attain the rank of a completely perfect Buddha for the sake of freeing all sentient beings from suffering and causing all sentient beings to have happiness."

Cultivating this thought in meditation is the second of the three principal paths to enlightenment. If you are able, cultivate it. There is no greater benefit to yourself and sentient beings; even if you read all the books, all the scriptures and their commentaries, you will find that there is no more helpful meditation. There is none.

If you are able to cultivate it in meditation for a long period of time, of course there is great benefit, but merely understanding this presentation once is said to be of such great benefit that if we attempted to explain it, we would not finish for many thousands of aeons.

Also, with respect to myself, I have offered you a clear explanation of the second of the three principal paths in accordance with the explanation of the great Buddhist systems, and when I think of the value of having explained such to you, I feel that it would be difficult for the benefit I have received in this lifetime to come in another lifetime. The circumstances even for such talk are extremely rare.

So, when you meditate, you may do all seven steps; recognition of all sentient beings as mothers, mindfulness of their kindness, intention to repay their kindness, love, compassion, unusual attitude, and the altruistic aspiration to highest enlightenment, or you may concentrate on the unusual attitude, thinking, "I assume the burden of causing all sentient beings throughout space—as illustrated by my parents of this lifetime—to have happiness and the causes of happiness. I assume the burden of freeing them from suffering and the causes of suffering. If I did not attain Buddhahood I could not do this, therefore I will attain the rank of a Buddha."

Whether you cultivate this in meditation in the morning, evening, or any other time, or even if you do not find time to cultivate it in meditation, from time to time think, "I will join all sentient beings with happiness and free all sentient beings from suffering. In order to do that, I will attain Buddhahood. Once I have attained Buddhahood, I will lead them upward."

If you keep putting this in your mind such that you will not forget it, an incomparable state will arise.

If you have any questions, please ask them.

Q. Can we help other sentient beings before we attain Buddhahood?
A. You can. Once your motivation is this altruistic aspiration, everything you do will be unusual. You will be a being of greatest capacity. Your non-virtues will become smaller and your virtues will become greater. It is clear in Buddha's word itself that there will be many in this country who will generate this altruistic aspiration, practice properly, and seek to aid others. This has already begun.

In his hundred thousand and twenty-five thousand stanza Perfection of Wisdom Sūtras, Buddha clearly prophesied this. He said, "In the future, and then in the future, it will spread to countries in the North."

This meant that the Buddhist teaching would spread to Tibet and then to Mongolia. At that time, it disappeared in India. Then the scriptures say, "Then it will spread here." "Here" means back to India. Now that many Tibetans are refugees in India, many monasteries have been established. The Indians themselves are the donors, giving an acre to each monk, and now the four orders, Nyingma, Sakya, Kagyü, and Geluk, have all established monasteries. The Indians' feeling is that the Tibetans have brought Buddhism back to India, and the loss of it in their own country was a disaster. Thus, in between times, the teaching has spread back to India.

Then the scriptures say, "Two thousand five hundred years after my death, the excellent doctrine will spread to the land of the red-faced people." The land of the red-faced people is this land of America. It became America almost two hundred years ago, but before that time it was the land of the red-faced Indians. Two thousand five hundred years after Buddha died was the year 1957, and the dissemination of Buddhism to America began then.

Buddhism does not spread except to countries where there are many meritorious people, thus these are countries of wealth, where the people are intelligent, and learned—where food, drink and resources are plentiful and the country itself is comfortable and pleasant.

It cannot spread to a country where there is a great deal of suffering and war because in those conditions there is too much fright. Never mind practicing doctrine, one has difficulty even caring for one's own life. The doctrine cannot spread except to a marvelous country.

Such talk on the three principal paths to highest enlightenment is very rare; because you are very meritorious, it has occurred. Thus do not just engage in this altruistic aspiration during meditation, also think of it from time to time, "I will join all sentient beings to happiness and free them all from suffering. In order to do that, unless I attain Buddhahood, it will not be suitable. O, Three Jewels, please empower me so that I may attain the rank of a Buddha. I will explain the doctrine to others."

Think this again and again. You will know later that there is nothing more meritorious than this altruistic aspiration and the precepts which serve to induce it.

11

Wisdom

இண்டை

In previous sessions I have briefly offered you the thought definitely to leave cyclic existence and the altruistic aspiration to highest enlightenment. Now I will begin the correct view.

The correct view is an unmistaken cognition of the mode of being of all phenomena. The reason why we have been travelling in cyclic existence is that we have misconceived the nature of things. Thus, the correct view is very important. There are several different ways of asserting the correct view in the higher and lower system, the Prāsaṅgika system.

There is a correct view with respect to persons which is a person's mode of being or mode of subsistence and there is a correct view with respect to all other phenomena, that is to say, objects other than persons.

The correct view with respect to a person is a cognition of the subtle selflessness of a person and the correct view with respect to other phenomena is a cognition of the subtle selflessness of all other objects. These are abbreviated into the cognition of emptiness or the correct view.

If you realize such a correct view, then you cognize the unmistaken mode of being of objects. If you cognize the unmistaken mode of being of objects, there is no greater view to be realized. Because we have not realized it, we have travelled in cyclic existence.

Our misconception of the nature of objects is the basis of all our trouble. A false nature of things appears to our minds and not knowing that this is false, we—all sentient beings throughout space— assent to it and thereby wander in cyclic existence. Therefore whatever our teacher Śākyamuni Buddha and the former Buddhas taught was for the sake of cognizing emptiness. They taught emptiness directly to those who were vessels of direct teaching. And even if someone was not suitable to be taught emptiness directly, the practices which the Buddhas taught were only for the sake of cognizing emptiness.

Why is it that everything Buddhas teach is for the sake of cognizing emptiness? They did so in order that beings might abandon what is to be abandoned, liberating themselves from cyclic existence and attaining Buddhahood. Thus, in the commentaries of Buddha's word it is asked, "What is the measure of a person who has made Buddha's coming to the world purposeful? If a person forms an understanding of the correct view, then Buddha's purpose in coming to the world is fulfilled." Thus, if understanding is not formed with respect to the correct view, then the purpose of Buddha's coming to the world is not fulfilled. In essence, the actual purpose of Buddha's coming was the realization of the correct view, but even if this does not occur, those who generate the thought definitely to leave cyclic existence and the altruistic aspiration to highest enlightenment do indeed fulfill Buddha's purpose, but not in the way that a cognition of emptiness does. This is because the wisdom which cognizes emptiness is like a mother giving birth to the auspicious attainments in Hīnayāna and Mahāyāna, allowing abandonment of obstruction and attainment of the fruits of both vehicles.

Buddhas himself said that wisdom is the mother and method—that is to say, the motivation of seeking to leave cyclic existence or to attain highest enlightenment for the sake of all sentient beings—is the father. How is this? If one does not have the wisdom cognizing emptiness, then it is impossible to abandon the obstructions to liberation, as the Hīnayānists are seeking to do. Similarly, if one does not have the wisdom cognizing emptiness, then one cannot abandon the obstructions to omniscience and obtain Buddhahood, as the Mahāyānists are seeking to do. Thus, the strongest antidote for eradicating obstructions for all three vehicles—hearer, Solitary Realizer, and Bodhisattva—is the correct view.

If your motivation is to liberate yourself from the sufferings of cyclic existence and attain liberation, then that is called the method of a Hearer. Motivated by this thought, a Hearer engages in meditation on emptiness and attains the rank of a Foe Destroyer.

Similarly, a Mahāyānist's motivation is the wish to attain the rank of a Buddha for the sake of all sentient beings. A Mahāyānist engages in cultivating the correct view in order to abandon the obstructions to omniscience. With such a combination of method and wisdom, Buddhahood is attained.

For instance, in Tibet, Mongolia and so forth, if a mother had three husbands of different lands and gave birth to a son by each of the three, then the sons would receive the names of their father's lineage. Similarly, the correct view is like a mother in that it is shared by all three vehicles and it is necessary for their attainments. The different methods of the three vehicles are like the fathers, and in dependence on these methods, the difference in lineage and attainments arises.

The mother, the correct view, is common to all three vehicles in that it is utterly impossible to abandon the respective obstructions to the three attainments without it. Forming an understanding of emptiness is the best, but even if understanding does not form, and you only generate doubt or suspicion—wondering how persons and other phenomena are empty of inherent existence—the predispositions which cause you to travel in cyclic existence are torn to shreds. Or as another example, even if you had good new seeds of wheat or rice, they could not easily grow if they rotted. In the same way when emptiness is entertained, it becomes more difficult for the predispositions established by our former actions to produce cyclic existence. The force of mere doubt, wondering about the reasons for emptiness, is that great.

Āryadeva explains in his Four Hundred Stanzas on the Yogic Deeds of Bodhisattvas that if one generates the altruistic aspiration, thinking, "I will attain Buddhahood for the sake of freeing all sentient beings from cyclic existence," then, as I explained to you before, the benefits are as great as the limitless number of sentient beings throughout space. For example, a single sesame seed has only a little oil in it, yet if you squeeze a bushel of sesame seeds, then oil filling a large vessel will come out.

In the same way, when you generate this altruistic aspiration, thinking, "I will join all sentient beings with happiness and free all sentient beings from suffering," the benefits as limitless as space. If your field of awareness is all sentient beings throughout all of space, then the benefit will not fit in all the world systems; this is clearly said in scripture.

Therefore, even though you have not realized the correct view, you think, "I will generate the correct view and eradicate all suffering in order that all sentient beings might attain Buddhahood." Then Āryadeva says that the benefit is sixteen times greater than cultivating the altruistic aspiration alone.

Thus, even though you wish definitely to leave cyclic existence, if you do not have the altruistic mind of enlightenment, then aside from your own welfare, other's welfare is impossible on a large scale. However, even though you have both the thought to leave cyclic existence and the altruistic mind of enlightenment, if you do not have the correct view, then you cannot abandon obstructions and leave cyclic existence, never mind attain Buddhahood.

There are many ways to generate the correct view, but for beginners there are four essentials for cognizing emptiness. Through these four essentials emptiness can easily appear to the mind.

How are you to think in order to form an understanding of emptiness with respect to a person, yourself? You must first identify the opposite emptiness—the inherent existence which is negated with respect to a person—refute it, and thereby cognize emptiness.

Thus the first essential is to identify the object negated in the theory of selflessness. The way the opposite of emptiness appears to the mind must be identified. Let us talk about the way in which the "I" appears to exist in and of itself as if having its own nature and entity.

If you inherently existed, then you as a person would not just be designated to your mind and body, but would exist under your own power. You would exist in your own right. If a person did exist in its own right, then when a person, which is the object being designated, is sought, it would be findable. Is the head a person? Are the arms a person? Are the hands a person? Are the fingers a person, it cannot be found. However, we have not formed an understanding of the correct view, and, for example, over the past few days though we saw the body of a man, we thought the body of the man was the man. Although we might have seen the body of a cow, we thought that the body of the cow was the cow itself. That is the manner of our confused thought.

Actually, the body of a cow is the basis of the designation "cow" and is not a cow. The feelings of a cow such as its being hot, cold, comfortable or miserable, are not a cow; they are only feelings. The discriminations of a cow, such as, "This is tasty, this is bad, this is liquid, this is grass to be eaten," and so forth, are not a cow. They are just discriminations.

Similarly, the mind of a cow such as, "I should go over there," or "This is my calf, I should lick it," is not a cow.

Thus the name of a person is only designated to the collection of these five aggregates—forms, feelings, discriminations, compositional factors, and consciousnesses. Except that the person is only imputed in dependence on the mental and physical aggregates, the aggregates together or individually are not at all the person. In other systems of tenets, each of the five aggregates is asserted to be the person, such as the Cittamātra assertion that the mind basis of all (ālayavijñāna) is the person and the Svātantrika assertion that a subtle mental consciousness is the person. The fact of the matter is that individually the five aggregates are not the person and their composite is also not the person.

For example, when we see the body of a cow, we think, "This is a cow," but the body of a cow is not a cow. When we eat the meat, we are not eating a cow. We are eating the flesh of a cow. The composite of the physical and mental aggregates is the basis of the designation of the name "cow." After having done analysis, when you see the body of a cow, you will only think, "This serves as seeing a cow." You will not feel that the body of a cow is a cow.

Similarly, our own mental and physical aggregates are the basis of the designation of a human. The five aggregates of a human are not a human. Viewing our own mental and physical aggregates we are continually thinking, "I, I, I, I, I," with the sense that it naturally exists, that it can be pointed to with a finger. This thought of "I" is called the innate conception of "I". Without any study or training we have engaged in it since beginningless cyclic existence. Through this beginningless ignorance, which is the conception of inherent existence, we have mistaken the nature of phenomena.

When you cognize emptiness and supplement your cognition with the cultivation of love and mercy and the altruistic aspiration, then at the time of arriving at the first Bodhisattva stage you can easily give away your own body if asked. In fact, you will not feel pain yourself.

If we compare this to ourselves now, when someone asks, "Please give me your body," never mind our body, we could not even give away a finger. If a person pulled at our finger, we would become upset, thinking, "It hurts me." This is due to our misconception of "I".

In the past, Śāriputra—one of the two superiors along with Maudgalyāyana who are always depicted at Buddha's sides—generated an altruistic aspiration to highest enlightenment for the sake of all sentient beings. At a time when he had the altruistic aspiration but had not directly cognized emptiness, he was meditating and a non-Buddhist demon came near him and thought, "Oh, he is about to attain Buddhahood, I must destroy him." So he approached Śāriputra and said, "I am making offerings and need a hand. Please give me one of your hands," and he cried and bowed down. Because Śāriputra was a Bodhisattva and even though he had not directly cognized emptiness, he thought, "This is suitable," cut off one hand, and gave it to him. It hurt Śāriputra a great deal, but he thought that it had helped the man, and he returned to his meditation.

The demon came to see if he had destroyed Śāriputra's meditation, but he saw that it had become even stronger.

"Hey, he's getting even stronger. This is not right," he thought, and again approached Śāriputra. "I made a mistake about the hand. I don't need that hand. I need the other one. Please give me it."

Śāriputra allowed him to cut it off and take it. Returning to his meditation, he thought, "I gave one hand, now I have given the other one. How terrible the pain. Through this I can see how much suffering there must be for all the beings born in hells. How hard it must be for them to bear!" Thus his meditation had again increased, so when the demon came to check, he was again disgusted.

"Hey, I took both his hands and still have not been able to destroy his meditation. It has become much stronger." He cried and hit his head on the ground, shouting, "He has done a terrible thing to me!"

Śāriputra looked at him and thought, "I cut off my right hand and gave it to him, but he was not pleased, so I gave him my left hand, and yet he carries on like this. If I cannot help even one sentient being through giving my own body to him, how could I possibly help all sentient beings? I will not be a Bodhisattva." Thus Śāriputra fell back to the level of a Hearer. What was at fault?

He had not cognized the emptiness of inherent existence of his own body. Due to that, when he cut his body, it hurt and he thought, "Even if I mutilate my own body and it hurts, it still does not help." He was ruined through his own thought and made the causes for being reborn in a hell.

If the correct view is not directly realized, there is this fault. He had conceptually cognized emptiness, but had not attained a union of calm abiding and special insight cognizing emptiness. Even if he had not cognized emptiness directly but had achieved a union of calm abiding and special insight—cognizing emptiness conceptually—this would not have happened. The conception of inherent existence of his own body was too strong.

The attainment of the union of calm abiding and special insight cognizing emptiness is the beginning of the Mahāyāna path of preparation. Direct cognition marks the beginning of the path of seeing. If Śāriputra had arrived at the path of preparation, then his understanding of emptiness would have increased when asked to give his own body, and he would have been able to use the pain which he still had, due to not having cognized emptiness directly, to increase his compassion for sentient beings stricken with severe physical sufferings. He would never have fallen.

This is because calm abiding is an ability of the mind to set on an object as long as one wishes and special insight is an investigation into the nature of things. When a union of these two is attained, then there is no worry about suffering from mutilating the body, one's meditation only improves. When a union of calm abiding and special insight cognizing emptiness has not been attained and the body is mutilated, one gets worse, even forsaking an intention to help others.

Through cultivating again and again in meditation a union of calm abiding and special insight, you come to see emptiness directly, attaining the path of seeing and the first of the ten Bodhisattva stages. On the first stage the special perfection of giving is attained. Then it is possible to give away anything without worry about oneself or hope for gain and without any pain at all. There is no thought, "It will hurt," or "I cannot do this." This comes when emptiness is cognized directly because then you see that the mental and physical aggregates do not exist under their own power but through the force of contaminated actions and afflictions. They are only a means of assuming the suffering of birth, aging, sickness, and death; they are not a source of goodness. If someone needs them, you will give them, without regret. In time, you yourself will know the great benefit of directly cognizing emptiness.

Our meditation today is to identify the object of negation with respect to the person. You should identify the sense of a self-established, self-powered, inherently existent person, not just nominally imputed, but existing in its own right. Meditation on emptiness itself is meditation on non-inherent existence or the inability of phenomena to establish themselves.

Thus, at the beginning of your meditation today you should reflect on the need to generate a correct view realizing the mode of being of persons. Though the thought definitely to leave cyclic existence and the altruistic mind of enlightenment are principal paths, you cannot attain Buddhahood with these alone. You cannot abandon the wrong conceptions that need to be abandoned. Take refuge at the beginning, asking the Three Jewels for help in generating the correct view, "O, Buddhas residing in the ten directions, please help me to cognize emptiness. I will meditate on emptiness. Please enable me to meditate on and realize emptiness. Please help me to identify the object refuted in the theory of selflessness."

An emptiness is a negative of the object negated, which in relation to a person is the inherent existence of a person. For instance, when we say that a product is impermanent, we are saying that it is empty of permanence, that it is not permanent.

Similarly, when we speak of the selflessness of a person, we mean a person's emptiness of independence, a person's not being independent. You may feel that it is a waste of time to ask for help in cognizing emptiness rather than just cognizing emptiness. But this is not so. A cognition of emptiness is extremely important, and asking for help in meditating on emptiness establishes predispositions in the mind which, even if they do not ripen into an actual cognition in this lifetime, will do so quickly in a future lifetime.

A thousand Buddhas will appear in this aeon, and it is definite that at the time of one of those Buddhas you will cognize emptiness directly and attain the rank of a Buddha. This is very clear in scripture. Today you are beginning by establishing predispositions. Then with a subtle portion of mind, watch your own sense of "I" as if from a corner, without overpowering your consciousness through watchfulness such that the "I" does not appear. You may remember an incident in which you were falsely accused and had clear sense of an "I" who was helped. Cultivate this sense of "I". Watch it. See what it is like. See if it seems to cover a certain area which is its basis of designation. This is extremely important. Without a clear sense of the inherent existence that is negated in the theory of selflessness, talk about emptiness and meditation on emptiness are like shooting an arrow without knowing where the target is.

Please meditate.

12

Nāgārjuna

తుఁు

You have come here to think about the actual mode of being of phenomena. I will offer you a little of the history of his teaching. The four schools of Buddhist tenets—Vaibāṣika, Sautrāntika, Cittamātra, and Madhyamika—all present the correct view according to their own systems.

The best and highest of these systems is Mādhyamika. Within Mādhyamika there is a division into Svātantrika and Prāsaṅgika. We have been talking about the correct view from the point of view of the Prāsaṅgika system. Buddha set forth the system, and the protector Nāgārjuna was its specific disseminator.

Let me offer you a little of Nāgārjuna's story. In this aeon there will be a thousand Buddhas, and after the first, second and third had come, the fourth, our teacher Śākyamuni, was born. His father's name was King Śuddhodana. Śākyamuni resided in the capital of the kingdom until age twenty-nine. There he took a wife, had a child, and was appointed king in his father's place. During that time he completed his study of politics, but at the age of twenty-nine he became a monk. For six years, until the fifteenth day of the fourth—month of his thirty-fifth year, he engaged in asceticism. On the fifteenth day of the fourth month he showed the manner of becoming a Buddha.

We say "showed the manner" because according to the Prāsaṅgika system, he had attained Buddhahood aeons ago and was only showing the way in which Buddhahood is attained.

For seven days he remained silent and then Indra, the king of the gods, beseeched him to teach, and he turned the first wheel of the teaching at Varanāsi, on the fourth day of the sixth month.

He lived until his eighty-first year, turning three wheels of doctrine, setting fourth 84,000 bundles of teaching. Before passing away on the fifteenth day of the fourth month he said, "I have ripened those trainees whom I could ripen. The time of my staying in manifesto form as a Buddha has gone. You should practice. I am passing away."

According to the Prāsaṅgika system, Buddha's appearance in this world system and his passing away merely occurred to the sight of ordinary trainees for the sake of showing them how to practice. He did not newly become enlightened here. He was enlightened many aeons ago, and he came to our world system as a superior Emanation Body. This is the Prāsaṅgika presentation.

He appeared this way to common trainees so that even if they had not entered into practice in this lifetime, they would see that he had married, had a child, and done everything, and then had generated a wish to leave cyclic existence.

He showed the way of becoming enlightened so that people might know how to practice. If such and such practices are done, such and such an enlightenment will be attained. Once you are enlightened, there is no need to die at all. It is only to common sight that one does.

He thought that if he stayed and stayed they would not practice diligently; thus when he was eighty-one he said, "I have explained the practices that I need to explain. I will die."

At that time his trainees—the Hearers, Foe Destroyers, Bodhisattvas, Mañjuśrī, Vajrapāṇi and so forth—gathered and asked Buddha a question, "You are about to die. When you die, who will come to bear and spread your system? When will he come?"

Buddha said, "Four hundred years after I pass away from sorrow, a monk named Śrīman will be born in Vidharba in South India. He will also be called `Nāga'. He will spread without mistake the greatest among the many doctrines of Mahayana. According to common sight, he will be a first stage Bodhisattva, and afterwards he will leave from here and go to the Joyous Pure land. Then 900 years after I have passed from sorrow. Asaṅga will be born. He will explain the pure doctrine, and living for one hundred fifty years, will meet Maitreya, spreading Mātreya's Five Treatises in the world."

Nāgārjuna was the disseminator of the Mādhyamika system, and Asaṅga was the disseminator of the Cittamātra system. The greater of them was Nāgārjuna. He lived six hundred years, and his life was divided into three proclamations of doctrine. During his first proclamation of doctrine, Nāgārjuna became a monk at Nalanda and later as prefect corrected the wayward discipline of many monks.

Nālanda was a great monastery with forty-thousand resident monks. The monastery was a large town in itself. Much later the Muslims came into India and destroyed it completely just as the Chinese have destroyed Buddhism in Tibet.

Toward the time of the second proclamation, Nāgārjuna was lecturing to the forty thousand monks of the monastery. He could see two strangers who looked like humans at a distance listening to the lecture. When the monks dispersed, he went near where they had been standing; there was a fragrant odor. Later he saw that they were carrying something like incense in their hands. Thus one day he told the monks that when the lecture was finished, they should call the two strangers to him.

They came, carrying their incense, and when he asked, "Where do you come from? What is that odor?" They said, "We are Nāgas. When we stay with humans, their strong odor infects us with disease. Thus we carry this incense to prevent contagion."

"Where is your country?"

"It is at a great distance. Please come there. We have books from the earlier Buddhas, Krakucchanda, Kanakamuni, and Kāśyapa, and we also have books from the teacher of this era, Śākyamuni Buddha. We have the 100,000 Stanza Perfection of Wisdom Sūtra. When turbulent times came to the Mahayana, these books were taken to our land. We will escort you to our country."

Nāgārjuna said, "From among the many Perfection of Wisdom Sūtras we do not have the 100,000 Stanza Perfection of Wisdom Sūtra. Do you actually have it?"

"We definitely do."

Thus Nagarjuna went to Nāgaland and saw images and books of the former Buddhas and the extensive, middling, and abbreviated Perfection of Wisdom Sūtras of Śākyamuni. He taught the Nāgas, and they offered him the 100,000 Stanza Perfection of Wisdom which he brought back to India.

In his absence, the people wondered where the protector Nāgārjuna was. When he returned to India, in his place of birth, this was his second appearance in Vidharba, the first being his birth itself. Since he was absent so long, some nowadays feel there must have been a second Nāgārjuna.

Nāgārjuna's return to Nālanda with the books marks the beginning of his second proclamation of doctrine, during which he composed the Six Collections of Reasoning establishing emptiness as the final mode of existence of all phenomena. He thereby founded the Mādhyamika system.

Nāgārjuna also went to the Northern Continent later in his life and again returned to Vidharba, appearing there for a third time. He brought back with him the four scriptures which serve as the basis of Maitreya's explanation in his Ornament for the Mahāyana Sūtras.

Almost six hundred years into his lifetime, he was living near the king Sātavāhana to whom he had earlier sent his Previous Garland of Advice to the King and his Friendly Letter. The queen had not allowed their son to engage in the usual princely studies because the king had a karmic relationship with Nāgārjuna whereby he would live as long as Nāgārjuna lived; thus the queen thought their son would never have a chance to become king before he died.

Several of the boy's friends told him, "If you do not start studying the royal duties, you will never be able to assume the throne." The boy was very upset and asked his mother why he was not training in the royal duties. He asked his mother many times, but she just said, "That's all right, that's all right, don't worry about it."

Finally he became angry, saying to his mother, "I must become king, I am a prince. I am your child. If I do not study, I cannot take care of the kingdom."

His mother explained to him the father's relationship with Nāgārjuna. Later, he met with his friends who were all of the royal lineage and explained to them the reason. In time they all went to Nāgārjuna, bowed down, and begged him to die. Again and again they beseeched him, "Our royal lineage will be ruined. Please die. Let him become king."

Nāgārjuna had attained many special feats and thus was able to live as long as he wanted, but because they requested him so often, he wondered what he could do. Thinking over his past lifetimes, he remembered cutting the back of a worm with a blade of grass. He told the boy to bring a blade of grass, and the boy was able to cut off his head with it.

All princes and members of the royal lineage were very happy at Nāgārjuna's death, and it is said that from that time the monarchies in India began to weaken.

During his second proclamation of doctrine, Nāgārjuna established the Mādhyamika system. We rely on Nāgārjuna's books along with those of his student, Āryadeva. We also rely on Candrakīrti and Śāntideva, who clarified Nāgārjuna's thought. Buddhapālita wrote a commentary on Nāgārjuna's Fundamental Treatise on the Middle Way and Bhāvāviveka wrote in refutation of him. In turn, Candrakīrti refuted Bhāvaviveka supporting Buddhapalita and clarifying the Prāsaṅgika system as the true meaning of Nāgārjuna's thought.

Bhāvaviveka was indeed very learned, but in his Sautrantika-Svātantrika system, he explained that even though phenomena are empty of true existence, phenomena conventionally exist in their own right, whereas in Prāsaṅgika, if something exists in its own right then it necessarily truly exists. From this point of view Bhāvaviveka's system is not final.

If phenomena existed in their own right, they would not be dependent-arisings; they would not depend on causes and conditions or even their own parts for their existence. Such phenomena as here and there, the near bank and the far bank of a river, and you and I exist only in relation to their respective places of dependence. On this side of the river this is the near bank, but on that side, the other side is the near bank.

It is the same with east, west, south, and north. They all do not exist under their own power or in their own right; they rely on definite causes for their designation.

Why do we meditate on emptiness? All of our problems arise from the afflictions—our birth, aging, sickness, death, fighting, making war, discomfort when it is hot, discomfort when it is cold, hunger, pain from eating too much, and vomiting. This travelling in cyclic existence has a root, and if you are not able to destroy it, you cannot create happiness. Even if you made some progress it would be like winning one war but having to fight another. In order to stop the process of cyclic existence and the arising of the unwanted, you must destroy their cause. What is the cause?

The root of cyclic existence is ignorance. Nāgārjuna thoroughly understood thus. Ignorance is the view of this transitory mind and body as an inherently existent "I" and inherently existent "mine". The main purpose of meditation is to stop the arising of the unwanted; to stop the arising of the unwanted, you must stop its cause. Once its cause is stopped, the unwanted will not be produced. We rely on Nāgārjuna's identification of the cause.

A view of this transitory mind and body as a real "I" is the conception of yourself as inherently existent. Even though the conception of someone else as inherently existent is a conception of a self of a person, it is not called a view of the transitory collection as the real "I", which is the conception only of oneself as inherently existent.

The view of the transitory collection as inherently existent "mine" is the view that your head, your body, and your mind inherently exist. When these two are stopped, you will have left all the suffering of cyclic existence; you will have destroyed suffering. It is so.

How do we conceive ourselves to exist inherently? The bases of the designation "I" are forms, feelings, discriminations, compositional factors, and consciousnesses which are called the five aggregates. The "I", or the person, is the phenomenon imputed to the mind and body. Indeed, the "I" and the aggregates nominally or conventionally are one entity, and that is valid; however, we do not conceive the "I" to exist nominally or conventionally. We consider that it exists in its own right.

If the "I" and the mind and body existed in their own right, then they would be either the same or different. This decision that if the "I" and the mind and body inherently exist, they must either be one inherently existent entity or different inherently existent entities is extremely important. Without a decision that these two are the only possibilities, Mādhyamika reasoning would be inconclusive. If anything under consideration exists, it will either be one or different.

Car and house are different, and car and car are one. There is no third category. Our innate sense of an inherently existent "I" does not explicitly conceive the "I" either to be one with mind and body or different from mind and body. Our consideration here is that if the "I" existed the way it is conceived by the view of the transitory collection, then it would have to be either the same as mind and body or different from mind and body.

Last week you were investigating the object negated in the theory of selflessness—an inherently existent "I"—and this week you are investigating the conditions that would have to be true if the "I" existed this way. The purpose of these investigations is that ignorance causes all the suffering we experience in cyclic existence.

In your meditation today first set out what you are going to do. "I will cultivate in meditation the view that the `I' does not exist in its own right, that it is only imputed there by thought. O, Three Jewels, I petition you for help in developing the cognition that if the `I' inherently existed as it appears to do, it would be either one with mind and body or a different entity completely."

13

Are a Person and Mind and Body the Same or Different ?

ℭ℘ℐℴ

In the first stage of your meditation on selflessness, you recognized a person that inherently exist, naturally exists, exists in its own right, truly exists, actually exists, exists covering its basis of designation, exists naturally, exists in and of itself without depending on thought.

These are all hypothetical synonyms because in fact the person does not exist that way at all. If the "I" inherently existed, it would not depend on causes and conditions or even its own basis of designation. It would exist under its own power. However, this is yet to be discovered.

In the second stage of meditation last week, you reflected on the fact that if the person did exist the way it appears, then it would have to be either one with or a different entity from mind and body. This is because mind and body exist and the person exist, and you must have something to point to for each one of them if they concretely exist. Thus, if the person is one with the mind, then when you point to the mind—or you have a clear sense of the mind—you are pointing to the person. Or, if the person is one with the body or a part of the body, then when you point to that, you are pointing to the person. If the person were a different entity from body and mind, then you could point to the mind and body over here and point to the person over there, not necessarily in a different place, but at least susceptible to being pointed out separately.

Is it unreasonable in any way at all—if the person exists the way it appears, so forcefully, so concrete, as if it exists in its own right— that if you search for it, it should become clearer and clearer and you would have something that definitely is the person? Thus you made the determination last week that if the person exists the way it appears, it must be findable either as mind and body or as a different entity.

First, let us consider whether mind and body, which are the basis of the designation "I", and the "I", which is the object designated, are one. If the person is the same as mind and body, then since mind and body are two, the person would be two, or since the person is one, then mind and body would be one. In another way, consider the five aggregates—forms, feelings, discriminations, compositional factors, and consciousnesses. If the person is one with these, then since there are five, the person would be five. Or, since the person is one, the aggregates would absurdly be one.

Through this type of reasoning, enlarging it according to your own knowledge, you should come to a firm decision that the mental and physical aggregates and the "I" are not one. Then the only other possibility, if the "I" inherently exists, is that it is different from mind and body. The "I" would then be apprehendable separate from mind and body. In meditation clear away all instances of mind and body—the aggregates of forms, feelings, discriminations, compositional factors, and consciousnesses—and see if the "I" that originally appeared to have its own basis, its own inner nature, is apprehendable without mind and body. When you search for it, you will not find it anywhere. The "I" is not only not mind and body, but also not separate from mind and body.

To do this meditation you must search patiently for many months for the "I", using as your guide your own innate sense of "I" and then applying reasoning. In your investigation you will gradually develop a stronger and stronger sense of the unfindability of a concrete "I"; a vacuity will appear to you—not a vacuity of nothingness, but a vacuity which is the negative of concrete inherent existence.

Does this vacuity contradict dependent-arising? Not at all. Dependent-arising and emptiness are compatible. Dependent-arising itself is a sign that phenomena do not exist in their own right. For instance, barley, rice, and cabbage grow in dependence on causes and conditions; they do not appear through their own nature. An effect depends upon its causes for its production, and infact, a cause also depends upon its effect because independently it could not be called a cause.

Self depends on other, other depends on self; they do not exist under their own power. The far bank of a river depends on the near bank and the near bank depends on the far bank. They do not exist in their own right. Tall exists in dependence on short, short exists in dependence on tall. Big depends on little, little depends on big; they do not exist naturally.

High depends on low, low depends on high. Male depends on female, female depends on male. Thus, all phenomena depend on causes and conditions, on another phenomenon, or on their own parts for their existence. There is no phenomenon which is designated independently. This is the great reasoning of dependent-arising. It is the mode of establishment, the mode of being of phenomena. If you do not realize this and instead apprehend phenomena as if they exist under their own power, then your misapprehension of the nature of objects acts as the cause of wandering in cyclic existence.

This misapprehension is of two types, intellectually acquired and innate. Intellectually acquired misconceptions of the nature of phenomena derive from our belief in wrong systems of tenets. In dependence on these tenets we explicitly affirm the false appearance of concrete existence through citing reasons and scriptures. The innate form of the misconception of the nature of phenomena is inborn, existing with us from beginningless cyclic existence, without any study and without any explicit affirmation such as, "This inherently exists." we assent to the false mode of appearance of things as if they concretely exist, assuming their appearance to be true.

To take an easy example, we have in our own continuum an innate misapprehension of permanence. What is this? It is a manifest misconception of the nature of things such that, no matter how long we have lived, we still plan to do such and such tomorrow, this the next day, that the day after, this the next year and on and on, thinking, "I will do this, I will do that," without exactly thinking, "I am permanent, I will not die," but acting as if our basis were permanent.

If we analyze this, we will immediately understand impermanence. If we see that someone has died, we can reflect that we too are going to die, that there is no one in the world who has remained without dying. If someone asked you, "Are you going to die?" you would think, "Of course I will die," but usually we only think about our clothing, possessions, and activities, planning the various stages in which we will use them, not thinking that we will die. Although we are not saying, "I am permanent, I am permanent," the mode of our apprehension of ourselves accords with a conception of permanence and is called an innate conception of permanence.

When we look into it, there are indeed cases of babies dying in the womb or dying just after birth, or children dying in their youth before their parents; but when we do not analyze, then our thought is just that we will last forever. In the same way when we see someone whom we last saw six years ago, we think, "He is just that person." We do not realize that he has been changing moment by moment. We think that we have met just that same person.

Also, when we see an article that belongs to us, we think that it is the same as before. This is due to an innate conception of permanence. In the same way our innate sense of inherent existence misconceives the nature of "I" without explicitly using words like "inherently existing in its own right" and "naturally existing". Just as when we examine and discover the impermanence of persons and things we see them differently and no longer make plans with a sense that we will never die, so when we examine and discover the non-inherent existence of persons we will experience ourselves and others differently. Is the "I" the head? Is it the body? Is it the stomach? You will discover that this concrete sense of "I" is baseless.

You cannot say that the "I" is the body or feeling or discriminations or compositional factors or mind. Many persons cannot accept an "I" that is merely designated in dependence on mental and physical aggregates but is not findable among the aggregates. They feel that this would be nihilism; they cannot comprehend the compatibility of analytical unfindability and dependent-arising. For them, the two are contradictory. If something is a dependent-arising, then it must be analytically findable, they think. Therefore the Cittamātrins and Svātantrikas teach that when you search to find the person you finally discover a subtle type of consciousness that passes from lifetime to lifetime and is the "I".

For the Cittamātrins who follow Asaṅga, this is called the mind basis of all (ālayavijñāna). For the Cittamātrins who follow Dharmakīrti and for the Svātantrikas, this is a subtle form of the mental consciousness. They know that the person is not the eye consciousness, ear consciousness, nose consciousness, tongue consciousness, and body consciousness, that these are just the basis for designation of the temporary "I". They see that the body is taken to the funeral pyre or cemetery at death and does not go on to the next life, thus they say that the mind is the person. They cannot comprehend how rebirth and the cause and effect of actions could be possible when the person only imputedly exists.

These are examples of intellectually acquired conceptions of the inherent existence of "I". Their basic thought is that when the object considered is sought—such as a person or a table, which are imputed to mind and body and to the parts of a table—they are found, either as one among the many bases of designation, as in the case of a person, or as the composite of the bases of designation, as in the case of a table.

They say that the table is the collection of four legs and a top whereas the Prāsaṅgikas assert that the collection of the parts is only the basis of the designation "table" and is not a table. If the mind were the person and since persons are male and female, are there male and female minds? Do minds have the male and female genitals? Does a mind have eyes?

In the Prāsaṅgika system the person is the "I" imputed in dependence on the collection of mental and physical aggregates. This imputedly existent "I" is misconceived to exist inherently, as if it were concrete and findable. From beginningless cyclic existence until now sentient beings have been accumulating virtues and non-virtues, some being born as hell-beings, others as a hungry ghosts or animals, others as humans or gods. The reason for this is the misconception of the nature of things. Not considering persons and phenomena to be merely dependently imputed, we ascribe independence to persons and phenomena. Through this misconception of the mode of being, we take birth in cyclic existence. This is what must be abandoned.

How is the misconception of inherent existence abandoned? It is not abandoned through merely withdrawing the mind from such conceptions; it is abandoned through losing belief in inherently existent objects. This is why we are considering whether the "I" is the same as or different from the mind and body.

We first cultivated a clear sense of the appearance and conception of inherent existence; then we decided that if the "I" exists as it appears, it must be either one with mind and body or a different entity from mind and body.

Through analyzing these two with reasoning over a long period of time, we can lose our belief in such a concrete, findable "I" because if you cannot find it among mind and body or separate from mind and body, where can you find it? The conception of inherent existence is just like the conception of permanence—baseless.

We have been afflicted with this misconception since beginningless cyclic existence; therefore, a mere superficial understanding of non-inherent existence is not sufficient. We must meditate on it. We must cultivate the realization of emptiness of inherent existence until it appears clearly to our consciousness. Not only will long cultivation of this in meditation free you from cyclic existence, but it will also give you the ability to free other sentient beings from cyclic existence.

For the sake of having good intelligence when you are meditating, working, or associating with other sentient beings, it is helpful in general to petition the Three Jewels. In particular, it is very helpful to petition Mañjuśrī. I will explain how to petition Mañjuśrī.

All Buddhas abiding in the ten directions—north, south, east, and west, the four intermediate directions and up and down—have three great qualities: wisdom, compassion and power. Mañjuśrī is a physical manifestation of all the wisdom of all Buddhas in the ten directions. Avalokiteśvara is a physical manifestation of all the compassion of all Buddhas in the ten direction. Vajrapāṇi is the physical manifestation of all the power of all Buddhas in the ten directions. These three are called the protectors of the three lineages, and since Mañjuśrī is the physical manifestation of the wisdom of all Buddhas, the new attainment of wisdom by Bodhisattvas, their training in the high qualities of the path, their cognition of emptiness, their cognition of the three principal paths, their proceeding to the rank of a Buddha, and their effecting the welfare of trainees are all accomplished in dependence on Mañjuśrī. When Mañjuśrī is praised, he is called the father of all Conquerors. Our Buddha—Śākyamuni—and all the Buddhas of the past and those of the future did and will expand their intelligence and attain Buddhahood in dependence on Mañjuśrī.

For us who want to form an understanding of the correct view, who want to succeed in our studies in this life and in future lives and have good intelligence, the means is the recitation of Mañjuśrī's mantra.

At the beginning of a recitation you should say, "Homage to the lama and the protector Mañjuśrī, undifferentiable," and then recite his mantra, Oṃ a ra pa tsa na di ("phonetically": om a ra ba dza na di). A good time for recitation is in the morning when just awakening. Recite it as much as you can—a hundred times, twenty-one times, or seven times. After reciting it the number of times that you have determined, say, "Oṃ a ra pa tsa na di di di di di di," saying di di at the end as much as possible.

If you recite the mantra every day without interruption, in time over the years your intelligence will become far greater. You yourself will manifestly realize its effect. In the past, the Mongolians, living in Russia, Outer Mongolia, and Inner Mongolia, were extremely skilled in the Buddhist treatises. Their skill came from this mantra. As students, they were taught to recite, "Homage to the lama and the protector Mañjuśrī, Oṃ a ra pa tsa na di," after they studied and as they were going to sleep at night. It is very powerful for increasing intelligence.

I will now offer you the oral transmission of the mantra. Repeat after me:

Homage to the lama and the protector Mañjuśrī, undifferentiable
Oṃ a ra pa tsa na di
Homage to the lama and the protector Mañjuśrī, undifferentiable
Oṃ a ra pa tsa na di
Homage to the lama and the protector Mañjuśrī, undifferentiable
Oṃ a ra pa tsa na di di di di di di di di.....

Recite it at least one hundred, twenty-one, or seven times each day without interruption. If you do so for a long time, your intelligence will be very good. If the recitation is interrupted, it will not be as good. At any time when you have difficulty understanding a topic, pay homage to Mañjuśrī and recite his mantra for a while. It will help. You will understand its help. No matter where you go in the world, there are both intelligent persons and unintelligent persons, but in the past India was filled with Panditas, and the reason was that they achieved Mañjuśrī.

Thus, today when you meditate, you should think, "Despite the fact that I have been apprehending myself since beginningless cyclic existence to exist inherently, I do not exist inherently. In order to help all sentient beings throughout space, I am entering into meditation analyzing whether the `I' and its basis of designation, the mind and body or the five aggregates, are one or different entities."

Recite Mañjuśrī's mantra at this point and then reflect on the reasoning why the "I" can not be inherently one or different from mind and body. Through seeing that there is no concrete "I", you will understand that the "I" is a dependent arising, arising through designation in dependence on mind and body.

14

Nothingness is not Emptiness

ᏄᏇᎧ

Previously I have offered you cultivation of the correct view with respect to persons. Today I will offer the mode of meditation on the emptiness of phenomena other than persons.

Meditators of the correct view are of two types: those who have attained the paths of Superiors and those who have not. Those who have not attained the paths of Superiors are ordinary beings; those who have are Superiors on the paths of seeing and meditation.

If you meditate on emptiness without imbuing your mind with the meaning of selflessness, it will not serve as meditation on emptiness. How is meditation on emptiness done without imbuing the mind with its meaning? I will offer you a little explanation.

In the past, after Buddha's teaching had spread in Tibet, a degenerate form of Buddhism was propagated in Tibet by a Chinese monk called Ho Shang, and the Indian Paṇḍita Kamalaśīla was invited to debate with him. Kamalaśīla's teacher, Śāntirakṣīta, had previously prophesied the need to call Kamalasila to Tibet after his death. The reason was that the Chinese abbot Ho Shang would disseminate a method of meditating on emptiness wherein the meditator was not to think about anything. His view was that cause and effect and so forth do not exist, not non-exist, not both exist and non-exist, and not neither exist nor non-exist.

Thus this method was to sit comfortably without thinking anything. Why was one to think nothing? "Just as a white cloud blocks the sun, so a dark cloud blocks the sun," he said. In the same way both virtue and non-virtue obstruct realization of the unfabricated reality. He had sources for his teaching from sūtra, but he did not realize their proper application in the stages of the path.

Kamalaśīla was invited to Tibet according to Śāntirakṣita's word, debated with Ho Shang, and defeated him, restoring Buddha's own system in the land of snowy Tibet. He is the writer of the Three Stages of Meditation which are so widely renowned in Tibet. The conditions of the debate were such that when the Chinese monk lost, he had to leave the country—the system of the victor being adopted by the country as a whole. He left, taking all of his belongings with him except one shoe and some articles.

Kamalaśīla, analyzing this, said that although it had been shown that Ho Shang's teaching did not accord with Śākyamuni Buddha's actual system, a little of his method of meditation would remain. Thus, later, even though Buddha's teaching thrived. Ho. Shang's system of meditating on emptiness was disseminated here and there throughout Tibet and China—not thinking about anything, not anything, just sitting comfortably.

However, not thinking about anything and meditating on emptiness are contradictory. This means that for us ordinary persons, in our mode of meditation on emptiness, if an understanding of emptiness has not conceptually formed, it is impossible to meditate on emptiness. This is the thought of Kamalaśīla, Nāgārjuna, and Buddha himself.

We should distinguish between the manifest mode of meditation on emptiness of a Superior and the non-manifest mode of meditation on emptiness by a non-Superior.

What is the manifest mode of meditation on emptiness? It is a direct cognition of emptiness in which the wisdom consciousness cognizing emptiness and emptiness itself are like fresh water poured into fresh water, undifferentiable. It is called the space-like meditative equipoise. For us who have not attained the path of a Superior, emptiness appears in a non-manifest manner. This means that a generic image of emptiness appears to thought when an understanding has formed. What is a generic image?

For instance, if you close your eyes and think of your house, an image of your house will appear to you. Or, if you close your eyes and think about the shape of New York City, an image of New York will appear to your mind; you will not be seeing it with your eyes. Or, if you think about the car that you came in today, you will not see your car directly, but a generic image of it will appear to the mind. It is through such a generic image of emptiness that inferential consciousness cognizes emptiness, since we have not yet achieved a yogic direct cognition of emptiness.

Becoming accustomed to emptiness through the medium of an image, eventually we will cognize it directly, as if we were seeing it with our own eyes. At that point the mind cognizing emptiness and emptiness are undifferentiable like water poured into water. We need this. However, since we are beginners, newly meditating on emptiness, we must form an understanding of emptiness.

There are two subtle emptinesses in the Prāsaṅgika system, the subtle emptiness of persons and the subtle emptiness of other phenomena. Last time I offered you the emptiness of the person. Today I will explain the emptiness of other phenomena.

When we speak of the emptiness of the person, we are referring to a person's non-inherent existence or non-true existence. When we speak of an emptiness of phenomena, we mean phenomena in the division of all phenomena into phenomena and persons; therefore, we are referring to the non-inherent existence or non-true existence of phenomena other than persons, their emptiness.

Primary among these phenomena are the aggregates of forms, feelings, discriminations, compositional factors, and consciousnesses, which are the bases of designation of a person. For instance, when you have the five aggregates of a cow—a cow's forms, feelings, discriminations, compositional factors, and consciousness—you have the basis of designation of a cow. When you see the form of a cow, you think, "There is a cow over there," and indeed, seeing the form or body of a cow does function as seeing a cow, but the form of a cow is not a cow. It is the same with a human.

Today instead of referring to the five aggregates, let us divide the basis of the designation of a person into the six constituents. They are the four elements—earth, water, fire, and wind—and space and consciousness. All beings having form have these six constituents.

The earth element does not mean just earth, it refers to the hard substances in the body, such as bones, hair, fingernails, skin, and so forth. Fire does not mean mere fire, but the warmth of the body. Water means the liquid elements of the body, blood, pus, urine, and so forth. Wind refers to the five types of currents in the body: the life winds, all-pervasive wind, down-ward-voiding wind, upward-moving wind, and heat equalizing wind. When these four elements and their potencies are in balance, then your body is healthy; when they are imbalanced, then disease sets in.

When the element of earth predominates, then it is difficult to move the body, to go, to rise, and so forth. When the water element predominates, water accumulates in the body, and if you do not take medicine, you will die quickly. When the fire element predominates, you suffer fever and its attendant faults. When the wind element predominates, you become excited and anxious. When these four elements are balanced, then it is easy to move back and forth, to maintain an equal temperature, neither hot nor cold, and to remain balanced mentally.

The space constituent is not the non-product space—the mere absence of obstructive contact—but the holes and empty places in the body, the passageways of the gullet, intestines, and so forth.

The consciousness constituent is composed of the six minds—eye, ear, nose, tongue, body, and mental consciousnesses. Among the six minds the chief is the mental consciousness. You should very carefully identify these six slowly over a long period of time in your own continuum. These are the bases of designation of a person, but are not a person. Only in the lower systems is it said that a consciousness—either a subtle form of the mental consciousness or a mind basis of all—is the person. Their feeling is that the mind has been travelling beginninglessly in cyclic existence, assuming mental and physical aggregates and discarding them, assuming more and discarding them and so on. Therefore, the person is the mind.

However, in this, the highest system of Prāsaṅgika, even the mind is a basis of the designation of a person and not a person at all. Otherwise, there would be many persons.

Taking these six constituents as your basis, you engage in meditation on their emptiness, their being empty of existence in their own right. The reason for this meditation is that due to misconceiving the nature of phenomena we have wandered in beginningless cyclic existence until now, suffering birth, aging, sickness, and death, birth, aging, sickness, and death over and over again as hell beings, hungry ghosts, animals, humans, demi-gods, and gods, studying and forgetting everything, becoming angry and making friends, over and over again. This is due to the fault of apprehending a mode of existence in phenomena which they do not have.

When you meditate on the emptiness of such a misapprehended mode of existence, then the root of wanderings in cyclic existence will be gradually and utterly destroyed. This is because conceiving that persons and phenomena exist in their own right is the root of cyclic existence; it is the basic ignorance giving rise to all other types of confusion, desire, and hatred. Through meditating on emptiness, opposing this false mode of apprehension of phenomena, you will realize that the conception of inherent existence is a perverse consciousness.

If you meditate on the emptiness of the six constituents with the motivation of achieving highest enlightenment for the sake of all sentient beings, you will attain the rank of a Buddha. If your motivation is not the altruistic aspiration, you will only be freed from cyclic existence. In either case, your meditation will be a union of wisdom and method. The cultivation of a wisdom consciousness cognizing emptiness is to be conjoined with the force of a motivation, either to obtain Buddhahood for the sake of all sentient beings or to attain liberation for the sake of freeing oneself from cyclic existence. In this case we are practicing the Mahāyāna motivation and therefore are engaging in meditation on the emptiness of the six constituents in order not just to free ourselves from cyclic existence but to attain the highest enlightenment of a Buddha in order that we may help to establish each and every sentient being throughout space in Buddhahood.

As before, you should meditate on the non-inherent existence of the six constituents through an analysis of whether any of the six constituents is the same as or different from its basis of designation.

First, ascertain a clear notion of the inherent existence of earth, water, fire, wind, space or consciousness within your own continuum. For instance, you could identify the appearance of a concrete findable skeleton. Then identify the basis of the designation "skeleton." A skeleton is composed of many bones and the collection of those bones is the basis of the designation, skeleton.

Or, examine mind. It is composed of six types, eye, ear, nose, tongue, body, and mental consciousnesses. The bases of designation of mind are six. Or, consider one moment of the mental consciousness. What is its basis of designation? You can divide it into three parts—beginning, middle, and end of a moment. These three are the basis of designation of a moment of consciousness.

Then realize that the phenomenon designated and the basis of designation must either be the same or be different if they inherently and concretely exist as they appear to do.

Is the skeleton the same as each of the bones? No, because then each person would have many skeletons or there would be just one bone. Is the mind the same as the six consciousnesses? No, because then the mind would be six. It is true that from a certain point of view there are six minds, but here we are searching for mind in general. We are searching for the concrete sense of mind which originally appeared.

Is a moment of consciousness the same as the beginning of the moment, as the middle of the moment, or as the end of the moment? If so, then there are three moments, or there are not three parts.

Then analyze to see if the phenomenon designated is different from the basis of designation. Remove all the bones of a skeleton and see if you can find the skeleton. Remove the six consciousnesses and see if you can find the mind. Remove the beginning, middle, and end of a moment of consciousness and see if you can find the moment of consciousness. You must then understand that skeleton, mind, and moment of consciousness do not exist as they appear and attempt to overcome your belief in this concrete appearance.

We do not state these reasons merely for the sake of making a superficial decision. First, we erected the target, our own sense of a highly concrete object on which we base our desire and hatred. Thus the very aim of such four-fold analysis is to realize and remain in a consciousness realizing that phenomena have no objective base, even though they appear to be so solid.

Like a magician watching his own creations but not believing in them, we should not believe in these false appearances. Through becoming accustomed to emptiness in the space-like meditative equipoise, we will gradually and eventually overcome both the conception that assents to the false appearance and the false appearance itself. You should cultivate this realization in meditation. Eventually you will understand that skeleton, mind, and moment of consciousness are dependent-arisings; a skeleton arises in dependence on bones, mind arises in dependence on six consciousnesses, and a moment arises in dependence on the beginning, middle, and end of a moment.

In this context "arising" does not mean produced. It means exist. A skeleton exists designated in dependence on the bones. Mind exists designated in dependence on the six consciousnesses, and a moment of consciousness exists designated in dependence on the beginning, middle, and end of a moment. Thus emptiness and dependent-arising are compatible; an understanding of the one helps an understanding of the other.

Please begin meditating on the emptiness of the six constituents going through the four essentials briefly, in four sessions every day. Ask for help from the Three Jewels in realizing the compatibility of emptiness and dependent-arising.

15

The Supreme Practitioner

ⵚⵓⵚ

Today I will offer in summary form the entire path of religious practice.

Within the Buddhist systems there are three paths, small, middling, and great. Practitioners are also divided into three in dependence on their capacities: small, middling, and great capacity.

Beings of small capacity are also divided into three types, small, middling, and great. A being whose capacity is the small of the small does not engage in religious practice but seeks only the happiness of this lifetime. Who are these beings? Hell-beings, hungry ghosts, and animals. Also, all those beings merely seeking the pleasures of this lifetime are persons whose capacity is the smallest of the small. They do not take refuge and do not engage in religious practice, only seeking the food, drink, and resources of this life, like bugs.

A being whose capacity is the middling of the small engages in both religious and non-religious means for the sake of attaining happiness in this lifetime. He studies, practices, works in a factory, even makes war, sometimes engaging in religious practice and sometimes not. However, since his motivation is aimed merely at the happiness of this lifetime, none of his activities can function as religious practice.

A being whose capacity is the greatest of the small does not mainly seek the aims of this lifetime, but realizes that no matter how long he lives, he must die and is liable to rebirth as a hell-being, hungry ghost, or animal and therefore mainly engages in religious practice for the same of attaining a happy migration as a human or a god out of fear and concern for the sufferings of the three bad migrations. Though he works for the welfare of this lifetime, he does not mainly do so. Concerned and fearing his own suffering in bad migrations and believing that the Three Jewels have the power to protect him from that suffering, he goes for refuge to the Three Jewels, listens to doctrine, ascertains it in thought, and meditates for the sake of attaining a future rebirth as a human or a god.

A being of middling capacity is not just concerned with the next rebirth; he is seeking to be freed from the endless round of birth, aging, sickness, and death due to contaminated actions and afflictions in the three realms—desire realm, form realm, and formless realm. He engages in religious practice seeking liberation from cyclic existence and the bliss of the extinguishment of suffering, the rank of a Foe Destroyer.

These are Hearers and Solitary Realizers. They are seeking only their own welfare, not thinking of their own parents or other sentient beings. They are seeking to experience a peace for themselves, realizing that if they merely attain the rank of a god or a human in the next lifetime, they will still be subject to rebirth in cyclic existence, even in bad migrations. They make effort at hearing doctrine, thinking about it in order to ascertain its meaning and then meditating on it for the sake of freeing themselves from the entire process of cyclic existence.

A being of greatest capacity does not stop there. He realizes his own plight in cyclic existence and extends this understanding to all sentient beings throughout space, seeking that it is also not suitable for them to undergo suffering. He thinks, "Though there can be great enjoyment in this lifetime, upon death nothing can help except practice. At that time I must leave all my property, gold, silver, and so forth, I cannot take my own relatives and friends with me; never mind that, I cannot even take my own body. Leaving all these, I must go alone. In the same way each and every sentient being throughout space must go alone. I must free myself from cyclic existence, but even if I freed myself all of them would still have this great fault."

Then instead of settling in the path of a being of middling capacity, he cultivates the path of a being of greatest capacity, "Even my own enemies are merely enemies in this lifetime; in a former lifetime they were my parents and like my parents were extremely kind to me. Even if they act like enemies now, in the future they will be my parents and will extend great kindness and protection to me. My own mother, father, family, and friends of this lifetime are indeed very kind to me, but when I consider the kindness of all persons over the span of lifetimes, they are all equally kind. It would not be suitable if they did not have happiness and if they were not freed from suffering."

Thus such a person proceeds on the path toward becoming a being of greatest capacity. Like a prisoner in a prison to be executed in only a few days, he seeks liberation from the miserable condition of cyclic existence. Then applying his understanding of suffering to all sentient beings are realizing the equality of all beings, he generates an evenmindedness which is a freedom from desire and hatred toward friends, enemies and neutral persons.

Having done this, he does not remain in a neutrality of ignorance, deserting and abandoning others, but realizing that each and every sentient being was his own mother in a former lifetime and will be his mother in future lifetimes, he reflects on their kindness. "They were extremely kind. First, I was formed in their wombs and emerged like a bug; they fed me, nourished me, clothed me, taught me how to talk, walk, eat, study, and live. If I had not had them as parents I would not have known how to talk; I would have remained like an animal although I looked like a human."

Then even when he sees a bug, he thinks, "Now except for taking the form of a bug, this person was my mother in a former lifetime and was extremely kind."

Then he generates the intention to repay their kindness, the love wishing sentient beings to have happiness and the causes of happiness and the compassion wishing sentient beings to be free from suffering and the causes of suffering. Then when cultivating the unusual attitude, he thinks, "I take upon myself the burden of joining all sentient beings throughout space—as illustrated by my own parents—with happiness and the causes of happiness and freeing all from suffering and the causes of suffering. I cannot do this now, and thus I must attain the rank of a Buddha in order to do so."

This is the generation of an altruistic mind of enlightenment. "It would not be right if I did not develop the power to help all sentient beings to have happiness and be free of suffering, therefore I will attain the rank of a Buddha. Once I have attained it, I will draw them all to Buddhahood." With this as his motivation he engages in meditation cultivating the correct view, realizing the nature of all phenomena, persons and all else.

This is the practice of a being of greatest capacity; therefore, in Buddhism there are three types of practice. The small aim at not taking rebirth in the next lifetime as a hell-being, hungry ghost, or animal and seek rebirth in a happy migration as a human or a god.

The middling aim at attaining the happiness of freedom from cyclic existence, and the great aim at establishing all sentient beings in the rank of a Buddha.

Any practice within Buddhism is included within these three types. There are no more. In the past in Tibet, during the second dissemination of Buddhist doctrine, the Indian paṇḍita, Atīśa, was invited to Tibet, and he taught the practices of beings of small, middling, and great capacity. Several Tibetans came to him and asked, "If we engage in practice for the sake of happiness in this lifetime, of what benefit is it?"

Atīśa answered "If you engage in practice for the sake of only this life, the effect is rebirth in a hell or as a hungry ghost or animal." Thus, if you engage in hearing, thinking or meditating, your motivation should be directed toward something deeper than this life alone. Death is definite and the time of death is indefinite.

There is no one who has managed to stay alive. At the longest we can live a hundred or so years, but at death the warmth collects from the extremities of the body, the outer breath ceases, and finally the inner breath ceases. Then the consciousness departs. If we are to take rebirth in a bad migration, first the upper extremities become cold, and we exit through the lower parts. Even persons who are not normally sick have tremendous pain at this time.

If we are to take rebirth in a happy migration, the lower extremities become cold first, and we exit through the upper part of the body. At that time nothing helps except our former practices. The door of entry to practice is refuge, and the door of entry to Mahāyāna is the generation of an altruistic mind of enlightenment.

The refuge of a being of greatest capacity is preceded by two causes; the first is concern for all sentient beings' cyclic existence, solitary peace, obstructions to liberation, and obstructions to omniscience. Cyclic existence is repeated birth in the six migrations, aging, sickness and death.

Solitary peace is the mere bliss of the extinction of suffering without perfecting oneself in order to help other sentient beings. The obstructions to liberation are the conception of inherent existence and the desire, hatred and confusion it induces.

The obstructions to omniscience are the false appearance of phenomena as if they inherently exist whereas they do not and the inability to cognize emptiness and the phenomena qualified by emptiness directly and simultaneously.

A being of greatest capacity is concerned about these four faults in all sentient beings and believes that the Three Jewels—Buddha, his Doctrine, and the Spiritual Community—have the power to protect all sentient beings from these faults. Thus concern over the four faults and belief that the Three Jewels have the power to protect sentient beings from these faults are the two causes preceeding the refuge of a being of greatest capacity.

The altruistic mind of enlightenment, the door to the Mahāyāna, is a wish to attain Buddhahood in order to free all sentient beings from suffering and to establish them in happiness and the causes of happiness. Whenever you engage in hearing, thinking, and meditating—whether the topic is love, compassion, impermanence, emptiness, or the thought to leave cyclic existence—your motivation should be the altruistic mind of enlightenment. Within this motivation you should request help from the Three Jewels.

This teaching of the mind of enlightenment, induced by love and compassion, is very rare in the world nowadays. It is almost entirely lost in Asia. No longer present in China or Tibet, it remains only a little bit in Japan and again in India, having been brought back by the Tibetan refugees.

There are to be a thousand Buddhas in this aeon, the fourth of which was Śākyamuni Buddha and the fifth will be Maitreya. It is said that those who hear, think, and meditate on this aeon. Buddha prophesied that two thousand five hundred years after his death, his teaching would spread to the land of the red-faced people, and I am not deceiving you when I say that I have faith that all of you are persons of great merit who are prophesied by Buddha to attain enlightenment in this aeon.

Remember to dedicate whatever virtue you perform while hearing, thinking, meditating, or engaging in giving, ethics, and patience to the welfare of all sentient beings. Otherwise, it will be lost in a moment of hatred. Dedicate it to the welfare of each and every sentient being throughout space. Then your drop of meritorious power will be mixed in a great ocean and will not evaporate through to your attainment of Buddhahood.

Even if you meditate on nothing else, cultivate this wish to attain the rank of a Buddha in order to free all sentient beings from suffering and the causes of suffering and to join all sentient beings with happiness and the causes of happiness.

You do indeed need to take care of your present life but it should not be your main activity; it will disappear very soon.

Do not make a mistake here. Although it is wrong to engage in religious practice only for the sake of this lifetime, it is proper to cultivate wishes that all the people of the world attain comfort and happiness in this lifetime.

Thus our meditation today is to cultivate the thought, "In order to establish all sentient beings—enemies, friends and neutral persons—in the bliss of Buddhahood, I will engage in hearing, thinking, and meditating and attain the rank of a perfect Buddha. Once I have become a Buddha, I will help all others to attain Buddhahood. In order to do this, I will cultivate in meditation the three principal aspects of the path: the thought definitely to leave cyclic existence, the altruistic aspiration to highest enlightenment for the sake of all sentient beings, and the correct view of emptiness, the mode of being phenomena of all.

If the benefit of such meditation had form, it would not fit into the whole world system. If you have any questions, please ask them.

Q. Since we are seeking to end the suffering of sentient beings, why should we be concerned if they follow a path leading to solitary peace?

A. When solitary peace is attained, it is very comfortable. The suffering of cyclic existence is gone. Without helping other sentient beings as illustrated by one's own parents, one merely remains for aeons and aeons in comfort. One's fingernails will even enwrap the body. The Buddhas rouse such a person saying, "Not only are you not fulfilling the welfare of other beings, but you have not even perfected your own aim. You must generate an aspiration to highest enlightenment."

Thus a Foe Destroyer must enter the Mahayana on the path of accumulation, whereas if, as a being of middling capacity, he had extended his understanding of suffering to other sentient beings and developed love and compassion, it would not have taken him as long to attain Buddhahood.

Among practitioners, he is poor, but compared with non-practitioners, he is better in that he is freeing himself from cyclic existence, but he is not helping his friends who over the continuum of lives have helped him so much.

Q. Can a teacher give his realization of emptiness to someone else?

A. Our teacher said:

Buddhas neither wash sins away with water
Nor remove beings' suffering with their hands
Nor transfer their realizations to other; beings
Are freed through teaching of the truth, the nature of things.

Buddhas do not clear away suffering with their hands nor do they wash non-virtues away with water; they cannot pour the realizations in their own continuum into others. They liberate beings only through teaching the paths of freedom, what to adopt and what to discard and what is beneficial and what is harmful. Liberation depends on your own practice.

Bibliography

ᑐᕤᑐ

(All references are to the Peking edition of the *Tibetan Tripitaka*
published by the Suzuki Research Foundation, Tokyo-Kyoto.)

Commentary on (Dignāga's) "Compendium on Valid Cognition," Dharmakīrti.
    Pramāṇavārttikakārikā
    Tshad ma rnam' grel gyi tshig le'ur byas pa. P5709, Vol. 130
Four Hundred Stanzas on the Yogic Deeds of Bodhisattvas, Āryadeva
    Catuḥśatakaśāstrakārikā
    Bstan bcos bzhi brg ya pa zhes bya ba'i tshig le'ur byas pa.
    P5246, Vol. 95.
Friendly Letter, Nāgārjuna.
    Suhṛllekha
    Bshes pa'i spring yig. P5682 Vol. 129
Fundamental Treatise on the Middle Way, Nāgārjuna.
    See *Six Collections.*
King of Meditations Sūtra, Buddha.
    Samādhirāja-sūtra/Sarvadharmasvabhāvasamatāvipañcitasamādhirājasūtra
    Ting nge'dzinr gyal po'i mdo/Chos thams cad kyi rang bzhin mnyam pa nyid
    rnam par spros pa ting nge 'dzin gyi rgyal po'i mdo. P795, Vol. 31-32.
One Hundred Thousand Stanza Perfection of Wisdom Sutra, Buddha.
    Śatasāhasrikā-prajñāparamita-sūtra
    *Shes rab kyi pha rol tu phyin pa stong phrag brgya pa'i mdo.*P730, Vol. 12-18.
Ornament for the realizations, Maitreya.
    Abhisamayālamkāra
    Mngon par rtogs pa'i rgyan. P5184, Vol. 88
Ornament of the Mahāyāna Sūtra, Maitreya.
    Mahāyānasūtrālamkārakārikā
    Theg pa chen pa'i mdo sde'i rgyan gyi tshig le'ur byas pa.
    P5521. Vol. 108.

Six Collections of Reasoning. Nāgārjuna:

    Fundamental Stanzas on the Middle Way Called "Wisdom"
    Prajñā-nāma-mūlamadhyamakakārikā
    Dbu ma rtsa ba'i tshig le'ur byas pa shes rab ces bya ba. P5224, Vol. 95.

    Precious Garland of Advice for the King
    Rājaparikathāratnāvalī
    Rgyal po la gtam bya ba rin po che'i phreng ba. P5658, Vol. 129.

    Refutation of Objections
    Vigrahavyāvartanikārikā
    Rtsod pa bzlog pa'i tshig le'ur byas pa. P5228, Vol. 95.

    Seventy Stanzas on Emptiness
    Sūnyatāsaptatikārikā
    Stong pa nyid bdun cu pa'i tshig le'ur byas pa. P5227, Vol. 95.

    Sixty Stanzas of Reasoning
    Yuktiṣaṣṭikākārikā
    Rigs pa drug cu pa'i tshig le'ur byas pa. P5225, Vol. 95.

    Treatise Called "Finely Woven"
    Vaidalyasūtranāma
    Zhib mo rnam par 'thag pa zhes bya ba'i mdo. P5226, Vol. 95..